SHADOWS WE RUN FROM

SHADOWS
WE RUN FROM

NELSON L. PRICE

BROADMAN PRESS
NASHVILLE, TENNESSEE

CONTENTS

PREFACE

No ballads or bumper stickers heralded my football heroics. I had one claim to fame—the longest touchdown run in Mississippi high school football history. This race into the record book came on a cold October night.

It was the first year our high school had a football team. The opponent was soon to be state champion. The excitement of our first night game was exhilarating. A driving rain chilled body and soul, making the ball hard to handle.

Early in the third quarter the opponent was on our one-yard line—where they stayed most of the night—when not in our end zone. Their big fullback started around my end, and that meant trouble. Not for him—me! Their offensive tackle, who later made All-Southeastern Conference with Louisiana State University, took me not only out of the play, but almost out of the end zone. I regained my footing just as one of our linemen tackled the ball carrier. The wet ball popped out of his grip. Looking up, I saw it seemingly hanging in midair. As I grabbed it and started to down it for a touchback, someone yelled, "Run." Being a dedicated coward, I was afraid that if I fell someone might fall on me. I decided the "run" plan was the right out.

Getting through the line of scrimmage was easy. No one knew where the ball was. Thinking I was in the open, I checked over my left shoulder and was tremendously comforted to find my shadow right behind me. With the help of my peripheral vision, I checked over my right shoulder and was shocked to find one shadow too many right on my heels. Panic!

I knew I could turn on my afterburner and run the hundred in about *fourteen seconds flat.* With that handicap, it would be impossible to out sprint my pursuer. My only hope was to fake him off. Therefore, I cut left—and he cut left. A cut to the right resulted in the same move by that ominous character who speedily stalked me. Left and right, for over one hundred yards, I sprinted until at last I breathlessly crossed the goal line. In the sanctuary of the score, I turned to see who had been chasing me half the night. Much to my chagrin, no one was within eighty-five yards. They all, like a herd of Brahma yearlings, were straining to see, "What's that fool running from?"

In sheer exhaustion I dropped my head. Then I knew what had happened and why even the hometown fans were laughing instead of cheering. There at my feet were the two shadows. The lights of the stadium had cast a cross shadow and both of them were mine. For over one hundred and five yards I had been trying to outrun my own shadow. That is competition at its best. Someone ought to write a ballad about that!

Reflection on that experience taught me a big lesson. It pays to set goals and identify shadows. It makes the race of life easier and more productive. Life's objective is to run to the goal, not from shadows. A line from an old pop song sums it up, "Accentuate the positive, eliminate the negative."

We run from many shadows in life. Each time I find myself in a circumstance I don't want to face; every time a fear haunts me, I try to apply that lesson.

Where there are shadows, commonly called problems, we do well to face them. As we identify a need and come up with a solution, the problem vanishes. If one insists on running from shadowy problems, his life goal is not likely to be reached.

Suspicions and illusions cause more fear and anxiety than all of life's real obstacles. "As a man thinketh so he is," stated Solomon the wise. Karl Menninger said that thoughts are more important than facts. Facts are fixed; but what we think can produce optimism or pessimism based on the same fact. Facts are important, but the thought associated with them is more so. Proper mental attitude is vital.

Goal-setting is essential to success. It is simply saying one should know where he is going before he begins the journey.

SHADOWS WE RUN FROM

1 CHOOSE YOUR MASTER OR MISTRESS

The Shadow of Goals

> Prove that you can control yourself and you are an educated man; without this, all other education is good for nothing.—Anonymous

> God shall be my hope, my stay, my guide, and lantern to my feet.—William Shakespeare

> No man can serve two masters: for either he will hate the one, and love the other; or else he will hold to the one, and despise the other. Ye cannot serve God and mammon.—Matthew 6:24

Mississippi played Texas in the Sugar Bowl on a chilly New Year's Day. Mississippi's Rebels were on the Texas goal line and were pushing hard on the Steers horns. Both teams had gone into their huddles. A frisky little dog ran onto the field and did a rapid reconnaissance of the ball with his nose. This bundle of energy was white all over except the last two inches of his tail, which was black. With coloring like that, one name was most logical. Someone on the sideline guessed it and called, "Here, Tippy!" He cocked one ear, looking in that direction. Immediately someone in the opposite direction whistled and he turned to check him out. Soon hundreds were whistling and calling. In bewilderment Tippy spun around trying to decide which person to respond to and which way to go. In his moment of indecision a swift official stole the dog's moment of glory by swooping him up and whisking him back into obscurity. His hour in the sun was over.

Tippy typifies persons today. There are many voices appealing for man's attention. Historically it has always been.

Genghis Khan said, "Follow me and I will give you the world."

Napoleon said, "Follow me and I will give you the world."

Caesar said, "Follow me and I will give you the world."

Hitler said, "Follow me and I will give you the world."

Christ said, "Follow me and it will cost you the world."

Sex says make me your god. Millions have. The idol is embellished and exalted. Dr. William Brown, of the United States Public Health Service, stated: "Eighteen million American teenagers today have constantly dangled before them these unwholesome sex symbols. Our language itself is mired in sexual context."

This preoccupation results in perversion and possessiveness. In a wooded area just outside a large metropolis a little preteen girl's body was found. The assailant had sexually assaulted her and, after savage treatment, killed her. The child's dad observed bitterly: "I wouldn't blame the man as much as the society which produces such men. It is a society that allows sex magazines on newsstands for kids to read; a society that measures Hollywood stars by their bosoms; and a society where the telling of dirty stories and the use of foul language is commonplace. These things produce sex perverts out of people who have the slightest abnormal tendencies."

The First Amendment was not intended to let pervaders of pornography peddle their product to yahoos who might sacrifice other little girls to the god of sex. The end product of sexual obsession is a decadent society. Dr. Unwin, a historian of Cambridge University, after making a study of eighty civilizations spanning four thousand years, concluded that a society either chooses sexual promiscuity and decline, or sexual discipline and creative energy. Dr. Unwin wrote: "Any human society is free to choose either to display great energy, or to enjoy sexual freedom; the evidence is that they cannot do both for more than one generation."

Work says make me your god.

Just as sex in proper perspective is right, so is work. Obsession is the cause of difficulty. Some persons become addicted to alcohol, others to work. Breaking the habit for the workoholic is almost as difficult as for the alcoholic.

The residences of many executives become branch offices instead of homes. The executives defend their excessive involvement by asserting that the best footprints in the sands of time are made by work shoes.

Dr. Gordon Bell of Toronto, Canada, observed: "The terrific forces that now dictate the tempo of modern industry are calling the time as to who will be healthy and who will not. Even men with great human resources can be enslaved by (work) addiction. We've more slaves today than in the time of Lincoln." Write on, Dr. Bell!

Work is a beautiful way to serve one's fellowman, but it is a cruel mistress for the person who makes it his god. It must be a means to an end and not an end in itself.

When one gains a proper understanding of the difference in success and failure, he can better balance his work appetite. The issue is faithfulness, not success. God never asks man to be successful, only faithful. This concept reduces frustration. If one expected success in achieving the following goals, he would be frustrated.

- Let every human being hear the good news of God's love.
- Bring every person to a saving knowledge of Christ.
- Help stop poverty, hunger, and starvation.
- End violence, crime, and war by calling men to repentance and forgiveness.
- End prejudice, bigotry, and arrogant pride by teaching people to love God and their neighbor.

The fact that one will never be successful in getting all those things done should not prevent a faithful effort.

Education says make me your god!

Education is an admirable vehicle, but an unworthy destination. Every wise student will study as best he can. Each practical student should attain the highest academic degree of which he is capable. Ringing the bell in the classroom is sound business.

Education as a servant is superb but as a master proves to be a tyrant. Congressman William H. Ayers, United States Representative from Ohio, commented, "We educate without religion and make clever devils of many." By taking morals and basic Christian teachings out of education, we have told the gelding to be fruitful and multiply. He can't.

Charles H. Malik, former President of the United Nations General Assembly, a native of Lebanon who has been honored by over forty universities in twelve nations, made the following observation about our nation's educational system: "The soul of the learned these days is quite empty—empty to the bare bones. The students will rebel, not knowing what they are rebelling against, although they think they do. For they have come to the great banquet of being, seeking food and fullness and have been turned away empty." He added: "Until the fear of God and the dimension of the spirit are fully affirmed at the heart and being of the university (and all schools), we shall see many more casualties among faculty and students. . . . Christ must come back to higher learning if higher learning and, therewith, man and culture, are to be saved."

In 1968 results were issued of a survey which had been made at the annual meeting of the National Student Association. Student leaders from universities across America were questioned concerning why our educational system is failing. The consensus was that it fails because it does not answer man's four basic questions:

Who am I?

Why am I here?

Where am I going?

How can I get there?

Jesus Christ says make me your God. His business is answering those basic questions. As the one who came to serve mankind, he makes a loving Master.

Setting a goal is sometimes called "goal psyching." Studies reveal that the nearer one comes to attaining a goal, the more proficient he becomes. This is often seen in athletics. In a close game, one of two evenly matched teams may get a break and take the lead. As the game nears its end, players produce better and a rout often results.

In light of this, one should set long-range goals. Lifetime goals are worthwhile, but achieving intermediary goals is also advantageous. One-year and five-year check-off goals are helpful in reaching the long-range goal. The driving, motivating standard is to keep short-range goals. By getting closer to them, one produces more efficiently. It is difficult to maintain peak proficiency in trying to attain a long-range goal. Maximum performance can best be sustained regarding an immediate goal. A new short-range objective that is obtainable can afford renewed motivating influence.

These intermediate and immediate goals must be properly understood as guideposts. They are not an end in themselves, but a means to an end. One's ultimate long-range goal is the end.

Persons who fail to make this distinction suffer successive letdowns. A student who considers graduation an ultimate goal is disappointed the week after because it failed to fulfill his maximum expectation. This principle is seen also in the child who craves and even cries for a bike at Christmas. Soon after getting it, he leaves it out in the rain while playing with some old toy.

Guideposts, immediate and intermediate goals, if properly understood, give a sense of fulfillment. They become stepping-stones, not rocks for stumbling.

To identify goals precisely in life gives peace amid adversity. When one knows God's ultimate will for his life, he quits shouting a demand to know why something happens and begins to ask how. That is, now that this has happened, how can it be used of God to help me reach my ultimate goal? How does this "work together for good"?

The big picture is often essential to gain that answer. The solution is found in "together." At most meals persons eat two deadly poisons—sodium and chloride. When these materials are blended as NaCl (sodium chloride) they form table salt and work together to produce good—flavor. Persons completing Bill Gothard's "Institute in Basic Youth Conflicts" are given a button with the letters "PBP-GINFWMY." They stand for "Please Be Patient, God Is Not Finished With Me Yet." Not only should others be encouraged to be patient with us, we must also learn to be patient in pursuit of our goal.

Goals once attained have a beautiful by-product. One result of a goal meritoriously attained is happiness. Frequently, individuals consider this elusive butterfly an end in itself. Much time and money is spent in the pursuit of happiness. A basic principle that emerges from the Sermon on the Mount as preached by Jesus Christ is that happiness is a by-product of a job well done.

Two examples explain this concept. Consider a football game between two old rivals. Your team has a safe lead as the clock ticks off the last few seconds. On your team is a player who has given his maximum in this victorious effort. In the game he has twisted an ankle, skinned a shin, bruised two ribs, sprung a wrist, has had two teeth loosened, needs six stitches to close a forehead wound, and is exhausted. As he comes off the field in this disheveled condition, he is one of the happiest people in town. For over two hours he has been engaged in fatiguing, hard work. He has not given one thought to happiness. His preoccupation has been with getting the job done—winning. Concentrating on doing his job well on each play was important. The by-product is happiness.

The student who stays up until 1:30 A.M. studying is not thinking about happiness—his eyes are burning too badly and his back aches. He is considering only the assigned test. He studies well. A few days later when the test comes back, he is elated because he made a good grade. He is happy. His happiness is a beautiful by-product of a job well done.

If we could each gain and maintain this attitude, it would result in greater efficiency and proficiency. In addition, the elusive butterfly of happiness would come more often to light on our heart.

On the mountain Jesus identified some mental attitudes which produce happiness as a by-product. The beautiful attitudes are worthy mental goals. He said the poor in spirit, those who are mentally humble, devoid of pride, will be happy. The meek, those who yield possessions and person to God without greed, will be happy. The merciful, those who forgive, give love, abandon bitterness, will be happy. The pure in heart, those whose drives are controlled by God, remain morally pure, will be happy. The peace-makers, those who seek to make things right, abstain from condemnation of others, will be happy. The hungry and thirsty, those who have wholesome spiritual appetites, without fits of inconsistency, will be happy. The mourning, those who are grieved by what grieves God, avoid callousness, will be happy. The persecuted for righteousness' sake, those who stand with him, free from compromise, will be happy.

Attitude goals are strategic. What attitude do you have about today?

There is an excitement involved in approaching each day with the mind set: "I've never lived this day before. It can be a day of delight." Thrill with the psalmist: "This is the day the Lord hath made, I will rejoice and be glad in it."

These attitudes do not suggest blindness regarding adversity and offenses. The attitude reputed to have been held by Marcus Arelius is worthy of evaluation regarding offensive persons. He allegedly began each day by repeating to himself: "Today I will meet many offensive people who will insult, offend, and injure me, but I cannot behave in this way for I am a man on whom the spirit of God rests."

Immediate action goals are essential. It is good to jot down one's intended goals for each new week. Identify what is to be accomplished during the week. These can be broadly defined.

In planning the intended daily goal be more definitive. Challenge yourself. Make the action assignment so heavy that self-discipline will be essential. The maintenance of balance is necessary in order to reach peak performance. Therefore, allow adequate time for each item and provide for proper nutrition and rest. A checklist can be very helpful in attaining daily goals.

It is helpful to list resources and personnel available. This knowledge enables one to be more specific and direct. The shadow of uncertainty detracts from a goal. The object is not to elude shadows, but to reach the goal. Stop right now and:

1. Identify shadows from which you have been running.
2. Outline immediate, intermediate, and ultimate goals to be sought.

2 HAPPINESS IS—A BEAUTIFUL BY-PRODUCT

The Shadow of Happiness

> Most people are about as happy as they make up their minds to be.—Abraham Lincoln

> Very little is needed to make a happy life. It is all within yourself, in your way of thinking.—Marcus Aurelius

> I am come that they might have life, and that they might have *it* more abundantly.—John 10:10

Count Leo Tolstoy, one of the greatest men of letters ever produced by Russia, ran from shadows in search of happiness. Once while going through an extremely difficult time (sound familiar?) he went for a walk into the depths of a great forest. There he found an old peasant sitting on a log, eating a meager lunch of blackbread. After sitting together for a while, Tolstoy said, "My friend, I have been looking for a happy man and I believe I have found him in you." Then Tolstoy inquired, "Where did you find such happiness?"

In that instant the old man became a tutor and the brilliant Tolstoy the pupil, as he mused: "Sir, I found it in the only place where you can ever find it in this troubled world. I found it in God. You find God, sir, and you will be alive and vital and happy."

Try an instant replay in part: "alive, and vital, and happy."

What a beautiful contrast this concept is with the findings of a recent national poll which showed that 51 percent of those polled think of their lives as being dull and routine. That means that one hundred million Americans are still in search of what Tolstoy found. Astounding! The same poll revealed that 60 percent of those over fifty years of age regarded life as basically without meaning.

Robert Browning said life was "an empty dream."

George Bernard Shaw called it "a flame that is always burning itself out."

E. V. Cook spoke of it as "a hollow bubble."

William Shakespeare declared it "a walking shadow."

Isaac Watts referred to life as "a long tragedy."

W. E. Henley compared it to "a smoke that curls."

John Masefield described it as "a long headache in a noisy street."

Don Marquis said it is "like a scrambled egg."

It was all those things and more for Tolstoy at one time. It is for many now. It can, however, change. The life of one who has found God is alive with expectation and purpose.

Many people feel life is void because they feel nothing much is happening. If one expects and looks for excitement, opportunity, and happiness, he can see it.

Blindness makes for blandness. One such person was Jean Lenoir, a cobbler who lived on an obscure side street in Paris, who wrote in his diary, July 14, 1789: "Nothing of importance happened today."

Just a short distance away a large mob stormed the Bastille that day and started the French Revolution. Lenoir was not expecting anything exciting and he was not disappointed.

The happy life has purpose.

Viktor Frankl, the internationally renowned Austrian psychoanalyst, wrote: "Life has meaning only if there is purpose, a life task. The more difficult the task, the more meaningful the life."

Many young people having the desire to struggle and no opportunity create a synthetic necessity to suffer. Given gifts they know they do not deserve, indirectly their pride is hurt. They have read about the nobility of the pioneers who suffered to achieve and their parents who survived the depression. As a consequence of youthful desire to suffer, the hippie culture emerged.

Inherently, every person needs a purpose, something for which to struggle. As a child, I watched tiny chickens trying to pip their shells and hatch out. In order to help them, I broke their shells and made it easy for them. They soon died because they were too weak. They did not gain the strength that consequents from the struggle of pipping the shell.

Find your purpose and enjoy the struggle to fulfill it.

The life of the one who has found God and is committed to him through Christ is fulfilled.

One large segment of our society has revived an old approach to attaining contentment. The Stoics of ancient Greece used the word *autarkeia,* which meant "entirely self-sufficient" to convey the idea of contentment. They envisioned the state of contentment consequenting from man teaching himself that he needed nothing and no one.

To reach this state the Stoic proposed (1) to eliminate all ambition and desire and (2) to eliminate all feeling and emotion.

Socrates evidences the first of these when he was asked who was the wealthiest man and answered: "He who is content with least, for 'autarkeia,' self-sufficiency, is nature's wealth."

The second of these concepts could be achieved, according to Epictetus, if one were to: "Begin with a cup or a household utensil; if it breaks, say, 'I don't care.' Go on to a horse or a pet dog; if anything happens to it, say, 'I don't care.' Go on to yourself, and if you are hurt or injured in any way, say, 'I don't care.' "

What kind of society results from this philosophy? What if no one cared about pollution, population explosion, war, crime, employment, hunger, or injustice? Stoicism failed because it was inhuman.

The apostle Paul converted the usage of the Greek word *autarkeia* and said, "I have learned to be content in whatever situation I am." How? By an awareness. He asserted: "I can do all things through Christ who infuses his strength into me."

Contentment does not result from eliminating ambition and desire, but from having the right ambitions and desires. It does not consequent from the elimination of feelings and emotions, but from properly directing them.

The life of one who has found God and identified with him, through Christ, is a happy life.

Jean Paul Sartre observed, "You will never find peace and happiness until you are ready to commit yourself to something worthy of dying for." With such things as the rapid spread of Satan worship, which has resulted in violent murders; international military pressure resulting in political confrontation; national fragmentation between races, sexes, and ages resulting in explosive hate; student protestation intent on destroying the establishment; complacency eating out the energies of patriotism; lethargy lulling the spiritually strong to sleep; and indifference serving as the subtle sentinel to keep one from acting responsibly—chances are fair that one might get a chance to die for a cause. Be sure it is worthy of dying for.

In response to the old man Tolstoy said, "My friend, I will seek after God until I find him." Tolstoy records how he soon gave his life to God, and God gave it back greatly enhanced.

The counsel of Tolstoy's graying tutor is still practical: "You find God, sir, and you will be alive and vital and happy."

3 GET UP OFF YOUR APATHY

The Shadow of Leadership

> Leadership: The art of getting someone else to do something that you want done because he wants to do it. —Dwight D. Eisenhower

> There is no necessary connection between the desire to lead and the ability to lead, and even less the ability to lead somewhere that will be to the advantage of the led. —Bergen Evans

> And if the blind lead the blind, both shall fall into the ditch. —Matthew 15:14

There is a dramatic deathbed scene in the movie *Viva Zapata*. The elderly Zapata is speaking his last words to his son: "Trouble is coming. Find a leader. If you can't find a leader, be a leader!" That challenge motivated the son to become one of Mexico's greatest and most colorful leaders. "Be a leader!" The idea still stimulates one's imagination.

Did you ever want to be a leader, but were afraid to be? The idea of leading is exciting. The act of leading is costly.

Ever since I led the Scout pack, of which I was a member, into a swamp I've had concern about leadings. We were supposed to go on a uniformed march. My shortcut short-circuited that.

To be a leader one needs to know what characteristics a leader possesses. Many conceive of a leader as the one who walks or stands up front. He is the one everyone likes.

It is commonly assumed that his popularity got the position for him.

A leader is one who knows where he is going and is able to persuade others to go with him. As a young scout, I was in charge, but I was not a leader. I was able to persuade others to go with me, but I didn't know where I was going. Knowing where you are going and persuading others to go are equal in importance.

It is estimated that one out of twenty Americans has leadership ability. That makes a leader a rare bird. This species of rare bird is seldom protected. The favorite game of an estimated five out of twenty persons is "Get the Leader." This is the only way some people can assert their frustration. It is done to every leader from the President of the United States to the Chairman of the Better Bungler's Bureau.

A leader has to be tough—TUFF. Not hard, but tough. Glass is hard, but not tough. The leader who is tough, is flexible. The Occidental idea of strength is steel. The Oriental concept of strength is water. Water is flexible. It takes the form of its container. When an opening is given, water flows. Its consistent flow is forceful. It lifts, moves, and erodes obstacles in its path. A leader shows this kind of strength. He awaits his opening and exerts his authority. He is constantly ready and bursting with energy.

The leader knows where he is going. He is more concerned about getting there than anything or anyone. He cannot have rabbit ears attentive to the criticizing five out of twenty persons. The croaking critics are common and most often overly exaggerated. A true picture is more realistically like the farmer bothered by croaking frogs. He felt the din of their croaking was unbearable. Upon draining the pond, he found only two old croakers. The valley had amplified their effectiveness. A leader cannot be preoccupied with his critics.

When criticism becomes malignant, it manifests itself as gossip. In a good, unabridged dictionary the following descriptive definition of a gossip appears, "Gossips are older sheep who get alone together and rub one another's old sores." A leader cannot let a sick sheep distract or sidetrack him. The leader has somewhere to go.

An old baseball adage characterizes a good leader: "Stopping on third adds nothing to the score." A leader knows that only a finished product or project is productive. He not only wraps the package, he ties a bow on it. Completeness is the criteria for quitting. Tenacity of spirit is his talisman.

Giving up too soon is given by sales executives as the primary reason most salesmen don't succeed. An industrial survey revealed:

—48% of the salesmen quit after one try;
—25% stopped after the second try;
—12% gave up after the third;
—the 15% who kept at it made more than three-quarters of their sales.

Stick-to-itiveness is a must.

Some years ago, while attending the National Student Association meeting at the University of Indiana, I obtained a list entitled "Characteristics of a Leader." These elements are worth emulating. They are:

1. Innocence of a lamb.

2. Wisdom of an owl.
3. Cheerfulness of a cricket on the hearth.
4. Friendliness of a squirrel.
5. Calmness of a camel.
6. Diligence of a beaver.
7. Patience of an ox.
8. Adaptability of a chameleon.
9. Vision of an eagle.
10. Endurance of an elephant.
11. Tenacity of a bulldog.
12. Courage of a lion.

The characteristics to be avoided are:

1. Fuzziness of a lamb.
2. Monotonous hooting of an owl.
3. Frequent appearance on a hot spot like a cricket.
4. Acquisitive nature of a squirrel.
5. Haughty air of a camel.
6. Eagerness of a beaver.
7. Brute force of an ox.
8. Characteristic of being indistinguishable like a chameleon.
9. Ability to rob others as an eagle.
10. Thick skin of an elephant.
11. Bored look of a bulldog.
12. Ominous roar of a lion.

A leader should be more concerned with his cause than his person. Leadership affords no room for preoccupation with one's sense of importance. Fame and popularity, often associated with leadership, are short lived. An incident in the life of Calvin Coolidge illustrates this.

Coolidge practiced law in Northampton, Massachusetts,

before becoming President. He always walked to his office from his home near Smith College. One could set his watch by the time of his stroll. His route each day took him by the home of a friend named Hiram. For twenty years their greeting was:

Hiram: "Hi, Cal."

Coolidge: "Hi, Hiram."

Hiram: "Nice morning."

Coolidge: "Nice morning."

Coolidge's time-consuming political career took him away to the offices of Lieutenant Governor, Governor, then Vice-President, and, ultimately, President of the United States. After his terms in public office, he returned to his law practice in Northampton and to walking that same route.

Sure enough, Hiram picked up the conversation right where it left off.

Hiram: "Hi, Cal."

Coolidge: "Hi, Hiram."

Hiram: "Nice morning."

Coolidge: "Nice morning."

Then Hiram added:

"Ain't seen you around lately, Cal."

Coolidge responded:

"Nope, been away a spell."

The prominence of the presidency had not influenced Hiram. Neither had it infected Coolidge with egotism.

The leader must not have an ego problem. Dr. J. D. Grey once told me not to get the big head over compliments. He said those who inflate your head are often only making it bigger so it will be easier to hit with the bricks

of criticism. Keep a balance. The job is to lead. It is hard
to do if you have to keep bowing. Arnold Glason observed:
"A good leader must take a little more than his share of
the blame, a little less than his share of the credit."

The right attitude in leadership is vital. An oversimpli-
fied definition of a beatitude is a beautiful attitude. "The
Jaycee Journal" of the Mississippi Junior Chamber of
Commerce lists "Beatitudes of a Leader."

Blessed is he who guides instead of dictates,
    for he shall have cooperation;
Blessed is he who is humble,
    for he shall receive praise;
Blessed is he who saves another's pride,
    for he shall have friends;
Blessed is he who believes in the cause he serves,
    for he shall be happy;
Blessed is he who in controversy seeks out truth,
    for he shall judge justly;
Blessed is he who wins his point tactfully and arouses no
        enmity,
    for he shall succeed;
Blessed is he who forgives his enemies and is loyal to his
        friends,
    for he shall be loved;
Blessed is he who ignores gossip and searches out the facts,
    for he shall be respected;
Blessed is he who has faith in his fellow men,
    for it shall be justified.

Be a leader! That entails *prayer.* God promises that if
any man lacks wisdom he can receive it by asking for it.

Ask, for discerning wisdom.

Seek, that which is known to be right.

Knock, repetitiously to obtain the difficult.

If a person is to lead, he needs to know where he is going and decide how to motivate others to go. The following affords a good checklist.

What is to be done? Establish the objective.

How can it be done? Develop a program.

When should it be done? Determine a schedule.

Who can get it done? Evaluate the personnel.

How much will be required to get it done? Decide what it will cost in time, talent, and treasure.

Never take counsel of your fears. Put your faith in your purpose, personnel, and the power of God to achieve a worthy objective.

4 SOMETHING TO BELIEVE IN

The Shadow of Purpose

Be not simply good; be good for something. —Henry D. Thoreau

A wise man will make more opportunities than he finds. —Francis Bacon

The kingdom of God is within you. —Luke 17:21

On a warm summer evening a young boy knelt on the edge of a dusty Mississippi road. Looking up at the moonlit sky he prayed: "God, please give me a self to live with, a work to live for, and a faith to live by."

Those elements add balance to a life, but they seem to come in the reverse order. First must be a faith by which to live.

While driving by Columbia University in New York, a companion gestured toward the row of bars on the opposite side of the street and said:

"Every four years these pubs have a new clientele. When the freshmen come in, they are Republicans. The second year they return, they are Democrats. Their third year, they are Communist. By the time they are seniors, they are so confused, they don't know what they are. They are thirty or forty before they find something in which to believe."

36

That something in which to believe must be personified in someone. That one is Jesus. Jerry Stovall, former All-American and All-Pro defensive back with the St. Louis Football Cardinals, said it well: "A man cannot live by himself. Each person has to have a fellowship. A fellowship of believers in Christ, the greatest leader the world has ever known, is the best source of peace and happiness."

If that one, Jesus Christ, was willing to die on a tree for our sins, does it make sense to think he will get us out on a limb and let us down? I have never known one person who gave Christ a full chance in his life and was disappointed in him. He is worthy of our faith.

Faith is trusting God to help perform his will in your life. When Moses tried to do the job by himself, he failed. He could not even keep one dead Egyptian soldier buried. When he cut God in on the action, he buried an entire Egyptian army.

Faith is the bridge across which we walk from reliance on self to reliance upon the Lord; from a self-directed life to a Christ-directed life. Faith bridges the gap between anxiety, fear, and frustration on one side; and peace of mind, joy, and assurance on the other.

The second request, in that roadside prayer, was for a work for which to live. We often overlook the teaching regarding six days of labor and put emphasis on a day of rest. There is dignity in work. Even the Creator labored six days before resting.

A success syndrome seems to have sucked our society into a vortex of the sewer of frustration. The esteemed emblem of honor is often a well-manicured hand. Whereas, a rough, calloused hand is considered by many as a badge of dishonor.

What is your DQ—Dignity Quotient?

Different moral jobs do not have dignity inherent in them. The concept that every workman is worthy of respect evidently lacks public support. Sanitation department workmen do a job not normally considered to have dignity because it lacks importance. Importance? Let these men fail to show up for a couple of weeks and their strategic importance becomes apparent. If the job is not done, it soon emerges as just as important as the physician's job of removing the refuse of the body, a ruptured appendix. If either the physician or sanitation department worker fails to perform punctually and proficiently, undisposed refuse can produce putrification, disease, and potential death. One would cause death more rapidly, but the other just as surely. Both are constructive and essential. The dignity of labor deserves a fresh compliment. Many units of work are required to develop a society: sanitation and surgery, banking and building, counseling and cleaning, preaching and planting, entertaining and excavation, legislating and loading. The integrity of work deserves our accolades.

Henry Ford spoke in summary of success. "Success? Success is to do more for the world than the world does for you." That concept is correct but contradictory to prevailing ideas such as:

Prestige is the word.

Integrity gets little play.

Faithfulness is of little consequence.

Honor has nominal cash value.

Prominence is the key.

The third request was for a self with which to live. This is often a by-product of a faith by which to live and a work for which to live.

Self-confidence is another way of referring to a self with which to live. James Bender, Director of the National Institute of Human Relations, put together the following test. In taking it, check areas in which improvement is needed. Resolve to use your strong points and to strengthen the weak ones.

1. Do you walk with a firm step and an upright bearing?

2. Do you speak with a good clear voice?

3. Are you convinced that you can grow in ability?

4. Would you prefer a job with a future that does not pay as much as a "sure job" holding no opportunity for advancement?

5. Do you rely on your own judgment, rather than seek advice about everyday problems?

6. Do you believe you can make a contribution toward making the world a better place in which to live?

7. Can you be cheerful when others about you are depressed?

8. Would you offer a suggestion to improve the work of your department or office?

9. Does the care of your clothing reflect self-assurance?

10. Do you keep impossible daydreams in check?

11. Do you solve problems pertaining to your work rather than run for advice?

12. Do you doubt your strength to work harder?

13. Do you do something about your worries?

14. Have you laid out a plan for improving your chances

for promotion?

15. Have you learned a technique for keeping calm?
16. Do you "bounce back" after a failure?

To enjoy living with yourself, get yourself off your mind and your mind off yourself. Following is a recipe for misery that is guaranteed to produce a detestable self.

"Think about yourself. Talk about yourself. Use 'I' as often as possible. Mirror yourself constantly in the opinion of others. Listen greedily to what people say about you. Expect to be appreciated. Be suspicious. Be jealous and envious. Be sensitive to slights. Never forgive a criticism. Trust nobody but yourself. Insist on consideration and respect. Demand agreement with your own views on everything. Sulk if people are not grateful for the favors shown them. Never forget a service you have rendered. Be on the lookout for a good time for yourself. Shirk your duties if you can. Do as little for others as possible. Love yourself supremely."

Right actions as well as right attitudes are essential in order to have a self with which to live. Doing what one knows to be right, to the best of one's ability, results in a self with which to live. When a person's life is right with God and his work is done properly, peace with self is the result.

Profession and practice must be parallel.

Charles Atlas inspired many young men to exercise. It worked for him by turning a ninety-eight-pound weakling into "Mr. Muscles." The process began when a couple of bullies kicked sand in his face and stole his girlfriend. That very same day Atlas started exercising. The result was that he became "Mr. America." He suppressed the bullies, got his girl back—and made a million dollars!

How? Lots of people were in the physical culture business, but soon failed. Atlas put them out of business. How? His answer: "I was the only one who practiced what he preached."

When one practices (work) what he preaches (faith), the result is a self with which to live.

5 RATS AND REASON

The Shadow of Faith

> Fear knocked at the door. Faith answered. No one was there.—Mantel of the Hind's Head Hotel, England

> All of my theology is reduced to this narrow compass: "Jesus Christ came into the world to save sinners."—Archibald Alexander

> Now faith is the substance of things hoped for, the evidence of things not seen.—Hebrews 11:1

"The Pied Piper of Hamelin"—this was the theme chosen for an activity of the PTA. The spectacular presentation was to produce revenue to supply ample funds for organizational activities.

An energetic program chairman had scouted around town for someone to play the role of the piper. To qualify one had to be able to play the flute. An exhaustive search yielded only one fellow who could play the clarinet. That was considered to be close enough. He got the job.

My older brother was in the third grade and an object of my admiration. He broke his arm the day of the grand production, squelching his opportunity to be in the play. Though I was not yet in school, I was as large as my brother. The teacher urged Mother to let me wear the costume and play the role. This was to be my first public performance. Those who knew me best said that the costume and role fit perfectly—I was to be a rat.

On that mild spring evening parents draped sheets over tables on the school yard and filled them with covered dishes of goodies. The rats were put beneath tables in pairs. My partner had the countenance of a Norman Rockwell boy who looks like he is searching for a cane pole to go fishing. Festivities reached a zenith as the piper appeared. His lilting "flute" tones summoned little rats from beneath the tables. They closely followed the piper to a large, shallow ditch in back of the campus into which they dutifully jumped.

Two concerned mothers watched apprehensively for their little rats to emerge. Noninvolvement by their rats prompted them at last to approach the table beneath which their rascal rodents were supposed to be. Gingerly lifting the sheet, they found their delinquents crouched about one foot apart, munching on carrots, and staring at each other.

What was not known by either was that each mother had told her little rat to wait for the other to go out and on cue to follow him. Without a little motherly encouragement, they might still be munching goodies and staring eyeball to eyeball.

The shadow of the unknown had us frozen into inactivity.

There is uncertainty anytime one engages in an unknown or unfamiliar event. Many people never venture and, consequently, never achieve because of this.

Fortune magazine conducted a poll inquiring whether young industrialists would prefer security or opportunity. The poll revealed that 98 percent preferred security over opportunity. Security is the watchword of our hour. The surest way to success, however, is to reduce one's competition from 98 percent to 2 percent and compete with those who had rather venture than vegetate in a human-like terrarium.

Abraham is a classic example of one confronted by the unknown. He is reported to have gone into a land which he knew not. He did it by faith. Faith is the rapier that foils fear every time.

The Christian is often accused of having "blind faith." This implies intellectual suicide. The opposite is true. Christ exhorted his followers to "know the truth." The Christian experience is based on faith in facts. Though it goes beyond reason, it does not go against it. The Christian should put his entire mind into his preparation, his whole heart into his presentation, and his full life into his illustration.

We live by faith. Yet, some mock the idea of faith in God. One would never eat in a public dining establishment without faith in the cook.

We go to doctors whose names we can't pronounce. They give us a prescription we can't read. It is given to a pharmacist we never see. He gives us a pill we don't understand, and we take it—by faith.

Our paycheck is taken to an impersonal bank and given to a teller we don't know. In spite of all the recent reports of embezzlement we still have faith in banks and trust them.

These acts involve committal faith. Abraham had a more sure thing going in his venture into the unknown than we. Yet, he, as we, acted to displace the shadow of the unknown by faith in a known God.

To find that which is unknown, one always starts with the known. A mathematical example illustrates this. If 6A equals 12B, what does A equal? To find the unknown, start with that which is known.

Often God's will regarding an issue is unknown. Many people feel that getting alone and thinking is the surest way to get an answer. There is some merit in this technique, but there is also another way. If one does not know what to do about a certain matter, he does well to get busy doing the things he knows he should do. This involvement in that which is known to be good is often a stimulus to thought, enabling one to produce correct answers. Proverbs 16:3 amplifies this: "Commit thy works unto the Lord, and thy thoughts shall be established." DO IT.

6 HIDING BEHIND A CHEMICAL CURTAIN

The Shadow of Fear

> They conquer who believe they can. He has not learned the lesson of life who does not each day surmount a fear.—Ralph Waldo Emerson

> If a person harbors any sort of fear it percolates through all his thinking, damages his personality, makes him landlord to a ghost.—Lloyd Douglas

> For God has not given us the spirit of fear; but of power, and of love, and of a sound mind.—2 Timothy 1:7

Being the only male lifeguard at a girls' camp had me heady until an unexpected threat arose. There were over a thousand teenage girls at Mandeville Encampment on the shores of Lake Pontchartrain, and I had to guard their lives.

I got the job because I was tall and could wade farther than anyone else. Two lives had already been saved early in the week, when terrorizing news arrived that appeared to threaten all lives. An insane rapist was reported to have escaped from the nearby state mental institute. He was last seen headed toward the encampment. Now the bliss of being the only male among all these girls became a burden. They had to be protected.

Campers were not told of developments as they settled down for the night. A few older friends and I assumed responsibility of patroling the area. The minutes became hours. Eternity was capsuled into one night.

Armed with a croquet mallet and kitchen knife, I inspected a remote cottage deep in the woods. A twig snapped like thunder behind the building. Frozen in fright, I crouched against a corner of the building and waited as the suspect moved closer. My heart begged for exit through my throat as the footsteps neared the corner. We were now so close I could hear his heavy breathing. His hulking indefinable shadow lay before me. My self-protective instinct said yell and run, but my sense of obligation to a thousand girls said, "They will call you chicken if you run."

One more step now and he would be in striking distance of my raised mallet. Sudden movement on behalf of the shadowy figure caused him to emerge in the darkness. One swift, furious blow was delivered. There was a groan followed by a resounding thud as my victim collapsed. I had him. One blow and I felled him. Now his identity became clear for the first time. That well-placed lick dropped that thousand-pound mule right in his tracks. It wasn't the suspected rapist at all. It was some farmer's plodding old mule.

The real rapist was caught a day later about one hundred miles from our location. The mule was revived by daylight and all were safe. It was two days before I told anyone about the mule. It's still hard to tell.

> Fear had caused a reaction,
> an overaction,
> and an improper action.

Fear always criticizes, ostracizes, terrorizes, and immobilizes. Fear prompts the urge to retreat or protect oneself.

Much of the mania associated with drug abuse is reaction

to fear. Drug abuse is many things. It is a chain smoker who can't kick the habit. It is a homemaker starting her treadmill with a diet pill for a quick pickup and turning it off with a sedative to induce sleep. It is a man unwinding with a few drinks. It is an eleven-year-old sniffing glue. It is a teenager smoking pot, or a hard core addict mainlining heroin. It is, above all, a threatened person seeking to retreat from stress behind a chemical curtain.

Drug abuse is an overaction to fear. Many youth warn adults not to use scare tactics in trying to prevent drug abuse. They advocate simply telling the facts. That is a yo-yo request because the facts are frightening. Marijuana is declared to be no worse than alcohol, and most agree. Likewise, cancer is no worse than leprosy, but what's so good about having cancer? Both are bad.

When alcohol is consumed, the delicately balanced body chemistry is disturbed in one out of every seven people who imbibe. With a drink, which drink no one can predetermine, enzyme disfunction occurs. The body cells demand alcohol. At that instance unwitting victims, who are retreating from some fearful shadow, run into the reality of being an alcohol addict.

Marijuana is the only drug known to give as great a high as before with reduced intake. With all other drugs, dosage has to be increased to get the previous effect. Clinically, it has been determined that the reason marijuana reacts as it does is because it imbeds itself in lung tissue and builds up. One elemental fact is known about foreign matter in the lungs—it causes lung cancer and emphysema. The retreating victim may avoid a frightening shadow, but he runs into the reality of a potential disease and an adversely affected motivational syndrome. That is, it reduces one's initiative and creativity.

Drug abuse is an improper action. Recently I visited my friend, the Chaplain of Bourbon Street, in his home parish. A contrast stood out. On the Canal Street end of Bourbon Street was the over-thirty gang. Booze and broads are their bag. Professional sex was on display and liquor flowed. On the Esplanade Street end of Bourbon Street was the under-thirty element shooting, puffing, and gulping their drugs while reveling in free love.

It was as though the Canal Street end crowd was pointing their index finger of accusation and saying, "Shame on you for using those drugs and engaging in promiscuous sex." The accused, on the Esplanade Street end, seemed to respond with, "Shame on you for using your drug and engaging in prostituted professional sex."

Both are right—or wrong! Both are improper actions.

The fear-casting shadow must be faced. Some biblical principles can help control fear.

Love dispels fear. It casts it out. Compassion for unloving, unlovely, and unlovable people removes their threat to us. Put a little love in your heart. Love is a sure cure for criticism.

Eight times fear is given as an emotion in Christ's followers' lives at the time of the crucifixion. "Fear not" was the message of the resurrected Christ, who was with them. An awareness of his presence with us helps to overcome fear. He is with the believer. Some days you may, in all honesty, confess to him that you do not feel that he is with you. At that moment, draw on the facts "I am with you," "I will never leave you," "I am with you always."

Pause and thank him for the fact that he is with you in spite of your feelings. The fact of his presence is a sure cure for ostracism.

Trust and confidence in the promised provisions of God give release from fear. He has promised to "supply our needs." If he watches over a sparrow, surely he watches over the apple of his eye—mankind. If he spared not his own Son, but delivered him up for us, surely he will meet our lesser needs.

Hurricane Betsy brought torrential rains and 200 m.p.h. winds to New Orleans. I found great comfort in reflection on a verse almost forgotten. It represents a swallow and a sparrow in conversation. The swallow inquires why human beings rush around and fret so. The sparrow responded:

> I think that it must be
> That they have no Heavenly Father
> Such as watches over you and me.

Trust is a sure cure for terror.

That leaves immobilizing fear. A knowledge of facts frees one from fear. Knowing what and how to do a task motivates one to act creatively. Therefore, know your resources, reserve, and recourse. Organize these factors and act.

Knowledge is a sure cure for immobilization.

7 ONCE MORE WITH FEELING

The Shadow of Failure

> There is no failure except in giving up.

> Our greatest glory consists not in never failing, but in rising every time we fall.—Oliver Goldsmith

> For God hath not given us the spirit of fear; but of power, and of love, and of a sound mind.—2 Timothy 1:7

The fear of failure has caused many people to forfeit life's race. It takes courage to compete. One has to be willing to run the risk of losing if he wants a chance at winning. There is no chance of succeeding without the possibility of failure. It is out of willing competitors that winners come. Those unwilling to take a chance are only assured of no success. Some of life's biggest successes have been achieved by the most unlikely competitors.

Ty Cobb jokingly accented the liability of a certain rookie's legs by referring to him as "Piano Legs." That rookie emerged, through struggle, as the "Iron Man of Baseball," Lou Gehrig. He set an all-time endurance record of playing in 2,130 consecutive games.

During his childhood, Sir Walter Scott was rated a dunce.

Napoleon Bonaparte had the dubious distinction of graduating 42 in his military class of 43.

Explorer Richard Byrd crash landed the first two times he tried to solo.

Zane Grey was fired by five newspapers.

Hume, the philosopher, was described by his mother during his childhood as uncommonly weak-minded.

Rod Serling wrote and marketed forty stories before he sold one.

Henry Ward Beecher, the preacher-philosopher, was spoken of by a teacher as a poor writer and miserable speller.

Walt Disney was released from his first major newspaper job because he "had little talent as an artist."

Louis Pasteur was written of by a teacher as ". . . the meekest, smallest, and least promising student in my class."

John F. Kennedy attributed his success to the fact that the Japanese sank his boat.

A young athlete's dreams faded when the Pittsburgh Steelers cut him. The Cleveland Browns promised him "next year," but they didn't come through. A year later, the Baltimore Colts did take a chance on him. In the fourth game of the year, the Colts were leading the Browns 20-14 when their quarterback broke his leg. The aspiring young quarterback went in and threw his first pass. J. C. Caroline intercepted it and ran it back for a touchdown. On the first play after the kickoff he fumbled and the Bears covered it for a touchdown. The Bears won 58-27.

Two games later against Detroit the rookie gained 324 yards passing—only to lose, 27-3.

He had a string of losses. Was he a failure? Knowing his name answers that question. His name is Johnny Unitas. Advantages can often be found amid adversities.

A boy in Decatur, Illinois, was very interested in photography. From a magazine ad he ordered a book on the subject. A publisher's mistake consequented in his getting a book on ventriloquism instead. A new career consequented from that mistake which gave birth to Charlie McCarthy for the boy Edgar Bergen.

More than anything, Whistler wanted to be a soldier. As a result of failing chemistry at West Point, he abandoned the dream. Later he jokingly said, "If silicone had been a gas, I would have been a Major General instead of an artist."

These persons accessed life's odds and assailed the assignment. They did succeed, but they had to first look the phantom of failure in the face, grin and go to work.

Twenty-five percent of any eigth-grade class drops out of school before graduating. Of these, 75 percent will still be looking for their first fulltime permanent employment five years later. They end up with such exciting jobs as night watchman at day camps. One told me he had a job as a diamond cutter. The next time I went to see the Atlanta Braves play, he was mowing the infield.

During this decade seven and one-half million youth will drop out of school. Many of them will be motivated to do so by fear of failure.

Mental attitude is a big cause of failure also. The Carnegie Institute once analyzed records of ten thousand persons and reported that only 15 percent of success is due to technical training. Eighty-five percent of success was judged to be based on personality. The primary personality trait listed was attitude. It was followed by thoroughness, observation, creative imagination, decision, adaptability, leadership, organizational ability, and expression.

The person with a cynical attitude will find something wrong about everything. He might hear that in 1955 Ted Allen of Boulder, Colorado, qualified for the World Horseshoe Pitchers Contest by heaving 187 of the two-pound missiles out of 200 around the peg. The negativist's likely response would be: "How did he do in 1956?"

"This is the age of cynicism. The 'in' people are all cynical. Only the out of it people are enthusiastic." A young, far-out student recently blurted that statement. Doing anything in the presence of a cynic is like bleeding in front of a shark. He will attack.

In extolling the virtue of cynicism, that student condemned a sure cure for a bad attitude—enthusiasm. Toynbee said, "Apathy can only be overcome by enthusiasm, and enthusiasm can only be aroused by an ideal which takes the imagination by storm." Everyone needs to find that ideal. I quoted that statement one Sunday, and my daughter said: "I am enthusiastic about school being out. That is an ideal that storms my mind." It did serve as a motivation for better grades in those last few weeks.

Walter Chrysler, a tremendous inventive genius, commented: "The real secret of success is enthusiasm: I would say excitement. I like to see men get excited. When they get excited, they break down opposition, they master defeat, they make a success of their lives."

Emerson observed, "Every great and commanding movement in the annals of the world is the triumph of enthusiasm." Failure retreats from the presence of this gritty giant called enthusiasm. It enables persons to overcome obstacles and do the impossible.

I recently renewed an acquaintance in New Orleans with a person I had not seen in over twenty years. This now successful evangelist reminded me that he had made his commitment to Christ in the first revival I ever preached. He noted that it was my enthusiasm over the gospel that impressed him initially. Then he asked, "I want to know, have you lost it?" Happily, I could reply that my contagious case had even gotten more acute and I likely would eventually relapse.

Enthusiasm even influences aging. Henry Thoreau noted, "None are so old as those who have outlived enthusiasm." Interpreted by this light, I have known some youthful sixty, seventy, and eighty-year-olds and some old sixteen-year-olds. The zest for living, created by enthusiasm, keeps one striving and achieving all through life.

Thomas Edison said, "When a man dies, if he can pass enthusiasm along to his children, he has left them an estate of incalculable value." The parent who does not face life with enthusiasm is robbing his child. He is fomenting failure by developing a bad attitude.

Enthusiasm! If it is such an asset, one does well to know what it is. Enthusiasm is a derivative of two Greek words, *en* and *theos*. *En* means "in" and *theos* is the Greek word for "God." Literally, it means the God within; actually, being full of God. When Christ's knock at the heart's door is answered with an invitation for him to enter, enthusiasm *(en theos)* consequents. Failure is no longer an issue. Faithfulness is the watchword. An energetic effort becomes the desire. The outcome is incidental. Thus, one's efforts become more bold and the victories more numerous.

The choice is Christ or capitulation.

Bill Bradley, the Rhodes Scholar, and NBA All-Pro, said it very definitively, "Let Jesus Christ come into your life. The choice is simple—

between the eternal and the passing,
between the strong and the weak,
between the living challenge and boring conformity,
between Jesus Christ and the world."

8 MIRROR, MIRROR IN MY MIND

The Shadow of Self-image

Most of the shadows of this life are caused by standing in one's own sunshine.—Ralph Waldo Emerson

We men are all thieves who have stolen the self which was meant as a part of God and tried to keep it for ourselves alone.—Joy Davidman

Ye should show forth the praises of him who hath called you out of darkness into his marvelous light.—1 Peter 2:9

Hypnosis has always intrigued me. Long before realizing there were potential dangers inherent in it, I encountered the mysterious Dr. Polgar. He was performing on campus at our school. Along with the other members of our basketball team, I sat down front. When it was time for "assistance" on stage my colleagues volunteered me. Dr. Polgar passed his spell on all six of us helpers and sat us on stools. I thought I was very conscious and rational when he told me he would put his hands on my head. On this cue I was to stand and crow three times like a rooster. My thought was, "I'll make a fool out of him by not responding." He put his hands on my head and made a fool out of me, as reflexively I stood and crowed three times.

Have you ever been hypnotized?

Some years later, my study of hypnosis revealed that one basis of hypnosis is confidence in the person administering it. In that light, we have all been hypnotized many times without being aware of it.

Exhibit A is my own experience. When I was in fifth grade, I considered my teacher, Mrs. Jones, to be the world's greatest. Greatest what? Greatest everything. I resolved that if I ever got out of fifth grade I was going to marry her. One day she paused by my desk, put her hand on my shoulder and said, "Nelson, you are a good little boy but you don't have any self-confidence." Wow! What a blow. She was the greatest and I had confidence in her. Thereafter, if I had shown any self-confidence it would have automatically made a liar out of her. I could not do that to her. Consequently, until my sophomore year in college my life was devoid of self-confidence. At that time thought conversion occurred in my life. With new understanding, acknowledgement was made that Mrs. Jones was as great as I thought and worthy of my confidence—but she was wrong. Whatever limited assets I embodied were a gift of God and confidence can be placed in God's gifts. For the first time in ten years I began to show signs of self-confidence.

Often now as I hear people say of themselves, "I lack self-confidence," or, "I am timid," or, "I am unlucky," a picture of some "Mrs. Jones" in their past emerges. Someone told them they were that way. Someone in whom they had confidence. Consequently, they have lived their life in the shadow of that hypnotic suggestion.

It is thrilling to see such a spell broken and a new self-image emerge. The sunlight of a new self-esteem can dispel the shadow of a negative influence. Pick your goal. No matter what people have said you have been or what you think you are, determine the image of what you can be. Write it down. What kind of an attitude do you want to manifest? What philosophy of life do you desire? How do you want to look? What do you want to achieve? What are your goals? Make a list. Once you have made your list, read your new goals out loud to see how they sound. If that is what you want to be, dedicate that person to Jesus Christ and spend the rest of your life in the joy of emerging. It is your cocoon, cut it. You were made to fly.

This new you should have balance.

On every continent Christ Jesus is revered as a great historical figure. Bill Bright, founder of Campus Crusade for Christ, spoke to the student leader of the early, Berkeley revolts. This young, card-carrying Communist was a Jew by birth and an atheist by belief. Dr. Bright asked him who was the greatest leader of all times. Reluctantly, he answered, "Jesus." Christ is a perfect example of balance. Luke said he grew "in wisdom, and stature, and favor with God and man." Four dimensions are thus defined: mental, physical, spiritual, and social.

Mental growth is a lifelong process. It is estimated by various psychologists that the average person uses only 10 to 20 percent of his mental capacity. Others speculate that 5 percent of the people think. Ten percent think they think. The remaining 85 percent had rather die than think.

The brain is a valuable asset. It weighs between 45 and 50 ounces. Almost 80 percent of this is water. The remaining 10 percent of grey matter has the capacity of storing over ten trillion units of information. That means the average human brain has enough capacity to store two and one-half million times more units of information than the most sophisticated computer. A bit of brain tissue the size of a pinhead can hold more information than any computer.

The brain is very much like a computer. In computer science there is an expression, "GIGO." It means, "What Goes In Goes Out." A computer has the capacity only of responding according to what goes in it. A human brain is basically the same. Therefore, a person should decide what "GIGO" stands for in his life. One extreme could be, "Garbage In, Garbage Out." Another choice is, "Gospel In, Gospel Out."

Mental stagnation can only be overcome by mental stimulation. The brain has a tendency to be lazy. Force it. Drive it. Demand of it. Let it know that it is depended upon. It becomes trustworthy when trusted, and dependable when depended upon. Read, memorize, and, in general, think lofty thoughts. Avoid such mind-globbing activities as watching too much television. There is no creativity in it.

Think about what you want to be. Plan what you want to do. Think these things out in detail. Some two thousand years before Christ, man concluded: "For as one's thinking is, such one becomes."

Physical development is a worthy goal. Diet is a vital part of physical growth. It is estimated that most Americans eat twice as much as is needed. That half which is not needed is believed to do more harm than the needed half does good. Do not overeat. It causes the mind to get sluggish. Blood needed for stimulating thought is required for digestion. Overweight makes the cardiovascular, skeletal, and respiratory systems work overtime. Every inch of fat over the heart is believed to shorten life expectancy by ten years.

Exercise is essential to good health. Walking is one of the very best exercises. It stimulates the thought process. Walking causes the muscles to knead the blood vessels in the legs. The action is very much like milking a cow. The heart pumps blood into one's legs and exercise activates its return. The next time you have difficulty thinking of something, go for a walk. Often the increased blood flow will increase one's recall capacity.

Exercise is good for the heart. Proper exercise reduces one's normal heartbeat per minute. The only rest the heart gets is between beats. If the count per minute can be reduced it gets more rest. This increases its life. Exercise for the rest of your life.

Spiritual growth adds balance to life. Two habits of Christ indicate what helped his spiritual growth. He frequently quoted the Old Testament. This reveals he engaged in Scripture memorization. A knowledge of the Bible is vital to proper balance in life. An awareness that the Bible does not ask us to do one thing that is not for our good, nor to abstain from anything except for our good, makes it fun to read.

Abraham Lincoln acknowledged: "I believe the Bible is the best gift God has ever given man. All the good from the Saviour of the world is communicated to us through this Book."

George Washington noted the importance of its scope: "It is impossible to rightly govern the world without God and the Bible."

One needs to know the words of The Man. To understand better and apply them one needs to know The Man of the Word.

Christ's second custom that served as a stimulus to his spiritual growth was worship. Repeatedly he is described as going to the synagogue "as was his custom."

Inadequacies within churches have caused many to abandon the practice of public worship. Karl Barth noted this. He also observed that these deficiencies are revealed at a proper time to embarrass the church and to prompt repentance. The church that constantly purges itself and calls for repentance and righteousness from its constituency helps persons grow spiritually.

Christ did not go to the synagogue because it was filled with perfect people. He went to be identified with God. I spoke for a week in services which a deaf mute attended regularly. Through an interpreter she told me she could not hear what I said. She revealed that she came just to let people know whose side she was on.

Social growth affords a beautiful blend in life. Jesus had a vigorous social life. His first public miracle was performed at the wedding feast in Cana. A dinner party was given for him in Bethany. A social visit, with spiritual dimension, was paid to the home of Zacchaeus.

One's social life should be designed to build friendships that afford wholesome influences. If one is found in repeated contact with an individual who influences him more for wrong than he influences that one for good, contact should be broken. The desired benefit from associations is to help each other. If a negative influence dominates, the person personifying positive attitudes should leave that negativist for a stronger person to influence.

Get a clear vision of your desired new self in the mirror of your mind. Make sure this new you has balance. Write a description of this balanced you. Seal it in an envelope and open it one year later. Check your development. Keep becoming the un-hypnotized new you.

9 THE EYES HAVE IT

The Shadow of Perspective

> Nothing contributes more to cheerfulness than the habit of looking at the good side of things. The good side is God's side of them.—Ullathorne

> If you think the world is all wrong, remember that it contains people like you.—Gandhi

> Rejoice in the Lord always, and again I say Rejoice.—Philippians 4:4

Think about it:

You are what you think.

You think what you are.

This, in part, helps to explain why people are so different. People who look alike are much more common than those who think alike. The principle causing this is called "Selective Perspective." Individuals, through life influencing persons, conditions, educational backgrounds, and total life involvement shape their personal perspective.

One's opinion of others is self-revealing. Harry Truman is credited with saying, "What Peter says about Paul says more about Peter than it does about Paul." That, in effect, was what Christ taught when he said: "Judge not that ye be not judged. For with the judgement ye judge, ye shall be judged." When one judges the motive in another person's actions, he is revealing what his own motivation would have been in that circumstance.

James wrote of God as being one "with whom there is no variableness." "Parallax" is a term used in physics for the Greek word translated variableness. It means one's angle of view. This can be dramatized by holding up the index finger at arm's length. With one eye closed, the finger appears to be in a certain spot. Without moving the finger, the open eye is now shut and the closed eye opened. The finger appears to have moved, though it has not. The angle of view made the difference.

Men often see the same thing from different parallaxes. Now consider the basic nitty and fundamental gritty: What is your frame of reference, your angle of view of life in general? We are so busy getting things done that we often fail to evaluate our personal philosophy. Following are two groups of thought representing different points of view.

Centuries ago there emerged in Western Civilizations two primary cultural philosophies: the Hellenistic and the Judeo-Christian. To understand them is to better understand each other.

The Hellenistic philosophy developed into maturity during the later Greek civilization and permeated the Roman Empire. It is divided into three schools of thought.

One is naturalism. The adherents think that if something cannot be seen, heard, tasted, felt, experienced, or proven, it does not exist. To naturalists the human mind must be able to understand a thing for it to be real.

The second school of Hellenistic thought is rationalism. It operates on the premise that man is a rational being. Rationally, two plus two equals four. Exponents of rationalism feel that, on the basis of reason, the issues of life should be added up as logically as two plus two. He reasons that given a certain set of facts all should reach the same conclusion. If you disagree with his conclusion, in light of the same facts, he is persuaded that you are entitled to your own stupid opinion.

The third school is humanism. Man is the basic measure of everything. Man sets his own values based on his presence. This man-centered outlook completely overlooks the true state of man. It assumes he is all good and all knowing.

The second Western cultural philosophy is the Judeo-Christian. It, too, has three basic schools of thought.

One is supernaturalism. Adherents believe there are things going on in our universe which the natural mind cannot sense or understand. The virgin birth and bodily resurrection of Jesus Christ are readily accepted as supernatural. The current occult craze represents a negative, or satanic, side of supernaturalism.

The second Judeo-Christian school of thought is that man is a spirit. Thus, man should make his basic decisions on the premise of spiritual needs.

The third Judeo-Christian school of thought relates to there being an ultimate authority. It is believed by these persons that there is one God and that he has given his authoritative word in the Bible. Persons of this persuasion feel that humanists have pushed man into the game of life and told him to figure out some rules for himself as he plays; whereas, he believes God has given life's rules in the Bible.

The basic difference between an athiest and a Christian is a thought. What think ye of Christ?

If you have had your Hellenistic eye open, try viewing through the Christian eye. Life takes on a new look.

Through the Christian eye, even on a cloudy day, you can see forever.

J. Edgar Hoover observed: "The pattern of man's thoughts necessarily is influenced by his fundamental belief. It has been my observation that those who believe in nothing, find life a thankless and unhappy quest; those who have faith, a spiritual pilgrimage."

10 ALLIGATORS AND OYSTERS

The Shadow of Adversity

> To the man who himself strives earnestly, God also lends a helping hand.—Aeschylus

> Many men owe the grandeur of their lives to their tremendous difficulties.—Charles H. Spurgeon

> When he giveth quietness, who then can make trouble?—Job 34:29

The pleasure of poling a pirogue down a narrow Louisiana marshland canal in predawn solitude is invigorating. Marshland beauty is antithetical to, but equal to, the breathtaking splendor of North Georgia mountains.

A kaleidoscope of sound is formed by geese honking, nutria squealing, ducks quacking, oil wells pumping, fish jumping, mosquitoes humming, and alligators bellowing. In the dark before dawn these sounds excite one's imagination.

This fascinating place is inhabited primarily by groups of America's most colorful citizens, the Cajuns. They are hardy descendants of the Acadians who gravitated to Louisiana from Canada and Nova Scotia. Their personality and physique took on the tone of this diversely fascinating marshland.

One colorful old Cajun there wears a necklace of alligator teeth. A visitor commented to him, "I suppose those are to you the same as a string of pearls to us." His wry response was, "No! Anybody can open an oyster."

The solitude of a duck blind gives one opportunity to think about that sound bit of philosophy. Anybody can do the simple—that which is easy. It takes someone extraordinary to do the exceptional. Anybody can open an oyster, but few want to wrestle an alligator.

An extra special person is required to stand up for a cause he is persuaded is right when he knows it is not the majority's cause. "Thus saith the majority," is a mandate for mediocrity. "Thus saith the gang," is a plea for permissiveness.

John Bunyan was more than an oyster opener. When offered his release from prison if he would stop preaching the gospel, he replied: "I will stay in this dungeon until the moss grows out of my eyebrows before I will make a butchery of my own conscience or a slaughter house out of my convictions."

William Penn asserted his alligator grip when he professed: "Right is right though all men be against it, and wrong is wrong though all men be for it."

The healthy heartbeat of a productive life is produced by a challenge afforded by competitive struggle. Without it, life is bland and bleached. Dr. John Calhoun reported on a three-year study in *Smithsonian* magazine. He placed two white mice in a nine-foot by nine-foot enclosure. He provided their every need and removed every threat to their existence. As the colony grew, he cataloged their behavior. In two years they numbered two thousand. At this point, a breakdown occurred in all organized structures of behavior. Soon the young began to separate and to destroy each other. They reached a point when they lost interest in everything except eating and drinking. Dr. Calhoun observed: "The mice really never learned how to mate or fight. Never fighting, never competing for mates, never protecting their young, they never knew stress. Most matured into blobs of protoplasm."

As one meditates on mice and men, many vivid distinctions are readily observable. However, there is a lesson to be learned—struggle is essential to survival.

For years the American dream has been of a material utopia of money, luxuries, job security, and social position. In the late 50's that dream nearly came true. In the 60's youth concluded that they had almost everything, but actually nothing. They had no struggles and were bored sick. Drugs and Eastern mysticism were tried as an unsuccessful escape. Escape isn't the answer. Stamina is, and struggle is its source.

Sir Walter Scott learned from lameness; George Washington, the patient statesman, from the snows of Valley Forge; Lincoln, the liberator, from his poverty; Disraeli, the crusader for fair play, from prejudices against him; Theodore Roosevelt, the disciplinarian, from his asthma; Edison, the inventor, from his deafness; Chrysler, the creative inventor, from the grease pit of a locomotive roundhouse; Robert Lewis Stevenson, the poet of pathos, from tuberculosis; Walter Judd, the surgeon-statesman, from his acne and skin cancer; Helen Keller, the inspiring example, from her blindness; and Jane Needham, author of *Looking Up*, from her iron lung.

Whenever one observes a great feat or hears of an inspiring achievement, he can be sure someone struggled. Michaelangelo's Sistine Chapel paintings is a case in point, as is Beethoven's *Ninth Symphony,* and Handel's *Messiah.*

Life is full of oysters and alligators. They are easily distinguished. They help to identify people and verify capacity. Every day each of us chooses between the two and our choices make us what we are. The next time there is a difficult, but potentially productive job to be done, choose your necklace. Anybody can open an oyster.

11 LAUGHTER: THE ELIXIR OF LIFE

The Shadow of Humor

> Men show their characters in nothing more clearly than in what they think laughable. —Goethe

> Remember that of all the creatures on this earth, only man has an intellect which gives him an immeasurable potential, and yet only to man has God given the gift of laughter. I believe that the latter was meant to compensate for the awesome responsibilities of the former. —Alfred Hitchcock

> He that is of a merry heart hath a continual feast. —Proverbs 15:15

Some people think humor is anti-intellectual. Instead, it is instant intellect. It evidences a capacity for immediate analysis and reveals a keen sense of observation. Persons with a good sense of humor are "polaroid"—they get the picture quick. Humor, though not the main course of life, is refreshing seasoning. Laughter is the loving hand of God on a troubled world's shoulder.

For the longest time, I was reluctant to use humor in public speaking because of the anti-intellectual connotation. Now, however, I believe our Creator intended us to have a sense of humor. I don't know if Adam had a funny bone or not, but he surely had a grand time with a spare rib.

A minister who preached from a manuscript failed to pick up the last page when he left his study for the pulpit. He was speaking on Adam and Eve. The church had a hyper-sensitive microphone and speaker system which picked up even the most whispered tones. As the minister finished his next to last page, he read that which now is printed boldly. Upon finding the last page missing, he murmured the rest: "AND ADAM SAID TO EVE . . . my soul, there seems to be a leaf missing."

Without humor in one's life there is something missing. One should not only learn to laugh, but laugh at himself. Only when we learn to laugh at ourselves have we developed a mature sense of humor. It's therapeutic.

Humor should never be used at the expense of someone else. Cervantes said: "Jests that slap the face are not good jests." "Our merriment must be of that kind which exists between people who have taken each other seriously," commented C. S. Lewis.

When asked what humor was, Will Rogers responded, ". . . almost anything . . . you happen to put . . . just right." Then he added, "But there's one thing I'm proud of—I ain't got it in for anybody. I don't like to make jokes that hurt anybody."

A sense of humor is a pole that gives balance to our steps as we walk the tightrope of life. In our pressure-packed time, perhaps a renewed capacity to relieve tension through being aware of the lighter, brighter side of heavy, dull issues might be the medicine to which the Bible referred that would do good like a medicine. It is God's gift to help prevent much emotional stress and nervous disorder. "A cheerful heart does good like a medicine, but a broken spirit makes one sick (Prov. 17:22). Lyman Coleman accented this truth: "Greater healing comes through hilarity—not heaviness." Rollo May, New York psychiatrist, amplifies this: "One with a sense of humor usually sees life steady and sees it whole."

A balanced sense of humor is a good goal. Forget about the shadow cast by false dignity and learn to laugh again. The rippling river of laughter is a blessed boundary between alert and inattentive individuals.

Give yourself this humor test.

Do you genuinely enjoy a funny story?

Do you enjoy telling funny stories to others?

Do you tell stories successfully?

Do you find stories easy to remember, with the punch lines coming through right?

Do people respond to what you think is funny?

The words "rejoice" and "joy" are two frequently used New Testament words. They are closely related to happiness, humor, and laughter.

The Scripture even says, "The Lord loves a 'hilarious' giver." Try giving yourself away to make him happy—and yourself.

12 I DIDN'T PROMISE YOU A ROSE GARDEN

The Shadow of Mastery

> Every man needs a master. Masterless men are like ships without pilots, or pupils without teachers, or soldiers without leaders. Some people rebel at this idea of having a master, as untamed horses rebel against the discipline of bit and bridle. But experience proves that there is no way to permanent happiness and success, no way of attaining a well poised personality except through discipline.—Henry Wade Dubose, *Christian Observer*

> It takes a lot of patience, and God—to build a life. It takes a lot of courage to meet the stress and strife. It takes a lot of loving to make the wrong come right; it takes a lot of patience, and God—to build a life.—Margaret Bradt Southmay

> And every man that striveth for the mastery is temperate in all things.—1 Corinthians 9:25

In running toward a worthy goal, the apostle Paul used a unique expression. He said, "I strive for the mastery." The beauty of the King James Version of the Bible is often as unintelligible to our twentieth-century ears, as our sports page will be to archaeologists two thousand years from now. Can you imagine them digging up one of our papers and finding that someone "burned the nets," or, that a halfback "spun off and ate up the turf."

In Paul's time his terminology was easily understood in athletic circles. The Corinthian Games were held every four years in Corinth. They were bigger than the ancient Olympic Games. Only the top athletes competed in this zenith of sports spectacles. Striving for the mastery was a concept which grew out of these games.

Every would-be participant had to prove his citizenship before being declared eligible. He must show indisputable evidence that he was a citizen of the Greek city-state he desired to represent. Paul's parallel is that if we want to compete in life as a Christian, we must prove that we are Christians—"Christ's partisans." One cannot represent someone he does not know, any more than he can go back some place he has never been. Citizenship in the kingdom of God is not a birthright but results from new birth. By faith, one lovingly responds to God's love offer. Upon asking for the gift of Christ's pardon of sin and pledging one's devotion to him, a person is given new life. One becomes a child of the King and is then allowed to participate in life's games as a representative of Christ—a Christian.

Next, aspiring athletes had to check into the gymnasium. This was not a casual thing, but a consignment of one's self to confinement inside the gym for ten months. No visitors or correspondence was allowed. He trained for a minimum of ten hours a day. This was an investment of ten hours a day for ten months. The hope was for a moment of glory. The anglicized Greek word for this period of training is "agony."

First-century Christians expected difficulty, deprivation, and even death as a result of spiritually striving for the mastery. Christ never promised us a rose garden. He never hinted that living for him was going to be easy—just right. Paul said:

> We know sorrow,
> Yet our joy is inextinguishable.
> We are handicapped on all sides,
> but we are never frustrated;
> We are puzzled,
> but never in despair.

We are persecuted,
   but we never have to stand alone.
We may be knocked down,
   but we are never knocked out!"
                2 Corinthians 6:10; 4:8,9, Phillips

After checking in the gym each athlete was assigned a personal trainer who had absolute control over him. The trainer was the one individual to whom the athlete was to respond most obediently. He was the one voice to whom the competitor was tuned.

While playing basketball in Brazil against the home team, which finished third in the Olympics, a most unusual development occurred. Thousands of enthusiastic supporters of the home team were in attendance. There was a fever about it all.

In the excitement and confusing furor of the opening tipoff, four Brazilian players instead of two lined up on their end of the court. This left my knobby shouldered, chicken-legged, collapsible-bodied self alone on the other end. Our 6'10" center tipped the ball to me. Being wide open on our end of the court, I dribbled down and stuffed the ball in with two hands. Though dunking was legal in America, Brazilians had never seen it. Time out was called and a volatile protest erupted. For fifteen minutes their fans booed and whistled. To them, it was unsportsmanlike not to shoot the ball. The game finally continued but so did the noise. The din was deafening. Yet, I was oblivious to it. There was one man sitting on the bench who could have spoken in a whisper and I would have heard him. We called him Coach. I not only tuned everyone else out, but I tuned him in clearly. He and I had the same vibes.

The spiritual equivalent to the trainer-coach is Christ. Many voices are vying for our attention. It is imperative that one tune into one. He doesn't ask us to do one single thing that is not for our good. His desire is to help us be a winner in life.

All competitors who checked into the gym trained nude. In practice they wore only a coating of oil. This was to lubricate the body and provide warmth. Oil was their only covering.

Throughout the Scriptures oil is analogous to the Holy Spirit. Christians, striving for mastery, must be under the Holy Spirit's influence if they are to compete successfully. He is available to every believer.

Each athlete did the same exercises. Boxers, marathon runners, sprinters, jumpers, and weight men all did the same exercises. There was no double standard in striving for the mastery. The same is true spiritually. What is morally wrong for a pastor, is wrong for a parishioner. What is right for a member, is right for a minister. The male and female, young and old analogies are true. Consistency is important.

Paul shifts his athletic metaphor to boxing. He asserted that he did not want to live like a shadow boxer. He wanted to fight real, not imaginary, opponents. These boxers fought for real. They wore only brass knucks. If one was knocked out, his opponent drew a line in the dust with his foot. Downed boxers were given a limited time to toe the line. When they did, the fight resumed. It ended when one was unconscious beyond recovery or dead.

Why would one go through agony in order to take a

chance on momentary glory or ignominious defeat? Why strive for the mastery? To win an olive crown! No. There was much more to it. Likewise, there is always more of a reward for Christian mastery than most know.

Each victor was publicly acclaimed and crowned at the games. He was then escorted to his hometown. A profile of his torso was cut in the city's wall. After he walked through, it was sealed with a different colored mortar so that his image would remain visible.

The winner was then driven downtown in a chariot. The world's first "flower children" lined streets along his route. Men tossed flowers and women sprinkled perfume on him.

The hero was then taken to the city square where a local poet read an ode written about him. His honor was preserved in verse.

The primary reward came next. The mayor presented him with a certificate guaranteeing free education for his children, plus lifetime income tax exemption. These were some motivating incentives encouraging athletes to strive for the mastery.

The rewards for competing as Christ's proxy, a Christian, makes it all worthwhile. Ultimately and inevitably life's race ends. Upon stepping through an old door called death one finds the best yet to come. The deceased disciple of Christ is then more alive than he has ever been. Best of all, upon reaching that goal the one who was willing to strive for the mastery will hear a "well done" from the coach.

13 MANNING THE "LIFE BOAT"

The Shadow of Church

> People do not live without worship—they die. They sink below themselves when they cease to worship one above themselves.—George A. Buttrick

> I am the church! In my sanctuary there is peace for tired minds, rest for weary bodies, compassion for suffering humanity, forgiveness for repentant sinners, communion for saints, Christ—for those who seek him. I am the church! Without me civilization must crumble! With me is eternity.—Author Unknown

> That he might present it to himself a glorious church, not having spot, or wrinkle, or any such thing; but that it should be holy and without blemish.—Ephesians 5:27

Church? How would you like to set fire to a sinking ship? The church seems to be a good one. Everybody is willing to fire a few volleys at the old ship of Zion now that she is listing port side. Consequently, many people are abandoning her. A declining membership, failing financial support, and its inability to solve all social problems, are sighted as examples of the futility of staying on board.

Recently I spoke at the Governor's Conference on Education in Atlanta. During a question and answer session which followed, a long-haired collegiate ripped into the church. My response was partial agreement with his castigation. That which later converted some of his thoughts, I learned, was my statement that "I do not believe it right to stereotype individuals or institutions. I have known some sorry long-hairs and some with exceptional character and ability. Likewise, I have known some anesthetized and anesthetizing churches and some that shocked me alive with excitement." The idea of individualizing persons was big with him, but the concept of considering churches independently was new. To speak of "the church" is as improper as speaking of "the car." Each is unique.

Because of an unpleasant experience in a church in the past, many people have become dropouts. As a result of finding a particular fellowship lifeless, others have given up on all. The thought that there might be a vibrantly alive, creative church has been discharged from the minds of many. A large segment of society has retreated from the church all together because of the public image of most institutional churches. It must be conceded that a stereotyped image of the church is enough to have caused most of us to want to run from her.

One factor that makes a distinction in churches was illustrated in my mind recently. We were visiting a glass blower's shop in Mamrea near Hebron, Israel, where the Lord appeared to Abraham. The furnace was heated to 2200 ° F. The molten glass was orange with heat. The blower pulled it out at intervals, placed it on an anvil and shaped it a bit with his sledge. He hit it hard and it never cracked or chipped. After his product was complete, it was allowed to cool. Once cooled, it then became brittle and delicate. When a church is on fire for the Lord, its constituents are moldable and strong. When the church cools off, its members become fractious and fussy. They have no spiritual strength and break easily under pressure. The church must maintain a zealous heat to create and attract.

Koinonia, one Greek word used for the church, refers

to a family. It means a partnership, a spiritual fellowship. The real church was intended to be a regenerating group of believers who have had a transforming experience before God. When the local church is such, there is growth, progress, and charm. The task of the church is redemptive. It is intended to disciple the nations, baptize them, and teach them in the warmth of a family-like fellowship. All churches have faults, but one that is fulfilling its role as a redemptive agent in a community will be blessed of God and is worthy of devotion.

Think about this. If you got in it, would it be better or worse? If better, it needs you; if worse, you need it.

The churches that are fulfilling their intended role today are growing as always. The church must grow, for it is an organism, not an organization, and organisms grow. Growth of the early church was a subject of an A.D. 150 writing referred to as "Letter to Diognetes."

The Christians are distinguished from other men neither by country, nor language, nor the customs which they observe. For they neither inhabit cities of their own, nor employ a peculiar form of speech, nor lead a life which is marked out by any singularity. . . . They dwell in their own countries, but simply as sojourners. As citizens, they share in all things with others, and yet endure all things as foreigners. Every foreign land is to them their native country, and every land of their birth as a land of strangers. . . . They are in the flesh, but they do not live after the flesh. They pass their days on earth, but they are citizens of heaven. They obey the prescribed laws by their lives. They love all men, and are persecuted by all. . . . They are poor, yet very rich. . . . To sum up all in a word—what the soul is to the body, Christians are to the world.

When those who comprise the local church assume this

likeness, that body attracts and projects. There is spiritual warmth and power. A church is to be the soul of a community, not the sole.

Tertullian, writing to the Roman Emperor in the second century, indicated the combustibility of a flaming fellowship. "We are but of yesterday and yet already we fill your cities, your islands, your camps, your palace, your senate, your forum, we have left only your empty heathen temple." They had put out the altar fires in the temple of Diana and lit the gospel torch even in Caesar's palace. That is one burning of Rome for which the Christians truly were responsible.

Justin Martyr echoed this second century sentiment in his writings. "There is no people, Greek or Barbaric, or any other race, by whatsoever appellation or manner by which they may be distinguished, however they dwell in tents or wander about in covered wagons, among whom prayers and thanksgiving are not offered in the name of the crucified Christ, to the Father." They had whispered the good news loud enough for the world to hear.

These early churches stuck to the fundamentals. Today criticism is given for doing so. However, the churches that do it still grow. Vince Lombardi, renown coach of the Green Bay Packers, is an example of one who stuck with the fundamentals of his game and produced a winner. The church that considers itself a divine institution intended by God to perpetuate such basic truths as the virgin birth, vivacious life, vicarious death, victorious resurrection, and valedictory ascension is still a vital fellowship. These fundamentals are the foundation of faith.

A group of birds decided to form a church. The duck

said, "Now we should require baptism by immersion."

"Oh, no," said the rooster, "because some people don't like getting wet all over."

The parrot contended that baptism was not important, but a good program was. Everyone clapped because they all knew a church has to have a good, rousing program.

The mockingbird asked about the organ. "No," said the thrush, "a piano is much better." The titmouse didn't want any musical instruments at all, and the sparrow was all for throwing out all music.

The goose stepped up and proclaimed that what was needed was a preacher who is good with young people. The bluejay figured that if the preacher would lay off sin and stuff like that, almost everyone would be pleased.

The real hassle came over the budget. Some said you ought to tithe—if you thought you could afford it, that is. Others thought they ought to do away with the offering and just have faith.

Finally, the owl arose and smoothed his feathers. Everyone grew silent for they knew he was very wise. "Brothers and sisters," he said, "all those things are secondary. What we need is sincerity." All the birds clapped and whistled. "Yes, sir," he repeated, quite pleased with himself. "Above all, we must be sincere—even if we don't mean it."

And so they formed their church and it was for the birds.

Faith in Christ is the cornerstone that characterizes Christian churches. Faith is suspect in certain "religious" circles but not in the scientific community. Plato declared that the best way to begin a work is to have faith. Bailey wrote: "Faith is a higher faculty than reason." Psychoanalyst Eric Fromm said, "Man cannot live without faith."

The internationally acclaimed scientist, Sir Arthur Compton, noted, "In every discovery I've ever made, I 'gambled' that the truth was there, and then acted in faith."

There is spiritual stamina and strength produced from proclamation of the "faith once delivered." The church proclaiming such truths is worthy of one's time and devotion. Most churches have among their members persons who could sell combs to Mr. Clean. Yet, when asked to serve, they get as nervous as a gnat in a bottle of DDT and list activities they are already involved in that make them as busy as a one-legged man at a kicking contest. They are nearly as confused as a termite in a yo-yo. "Seek ye first the kingdom of God."

Billy Rose said, "If you want to graze the sheep, you must take them where the grass is." Find a good undershepherd and he will provide good grazing. Join his flock.

My ambition for all churches was dramatized by a recent visit to the site of a church being demolished in our community. They had reached the stage of razing where the roof was off and the windows out. The radiant sun streamed in across the front, and beamed brilliantly where once the pulpit stood. A refreshing, soft, cool breeze moved through the open auditorium. Standing there I prayed, "Oh, God, may this be pictorial of more of your churches. Every time we meet to worship, may the glory of heaven shine in and may there be a refreshing spiritual breath for all." That kind of a spiritual experience revives one's spirit. That is the purpose of the church.

George Comstock, M.D., Professor of Hygiene and Public Health at Johns Hopkins University, revealed some physical facts that evidence church-going to be advantageous. He found, through extensive research, that persons who attend church regularly live longer, are happier, and have fewer tensions. That should be no surprise, after all, Christ said, "I am come that you may have life and that you might have it more abundantly." That fundamental fact is worthy of your faith.

> Abandon the church that believes
> Christ is no where.
> Get on board the one that believes
> Christ is now here.

14 LOVE BEARETH ALL THINGS

The Shadow of Inability

Dogmatism builds fences, love builds bridges.—Anonymous

Of all earthly music, that which reaches farthest into heaven
is the beating of a truly loving heart.—Henry Ward Beecher

Now abideth faith, hope, love, these three; but the greatest
of these is love.—1 Corinthians 13:13, ASV

As a twelve-year-old, I considered my grandad to be
superman. He had such a zest for life that it was fun even
to work with him. One summer workday involved building
a new fence. My goats and his cows had found too many
ways through the old one. We worked all morning digging
fence posts, setting the posts, and tamping them in tightly.
By mid-afternoon we had worked down to the corner and
stopped to take a breather. The entire rest time, that we
sat under a big shade tree sipping ice water, I was worried
about setting the corner post which came next. Corner posts
were always a couple of times bigger and much heavier
than all others. Thinking about having to pick up and place
that post caused me to sweat more than the actual work.

Finally Grandpa said, "Come on, boy, get a hold of
your end of the post, let's set it." Knowing the limitation
of my twelve-year-old muscles caused no little doubt about
my ability to lift one end, but Grandpa said do it and

he meant to do it. Grabbing on and straining, I was thrilled when the post cleared the ground. An overwhelming sense of accomplishment was accompanied by a surge of youthful egotism as we dropped that post in the hole. We did it!

It wasn't until about fifteen years later that conversation with an older friend caused me mentally to recreate what happened that day and to know how I did it. Obediently, I had picked up my end of that burdensome post, but when Grandpa picked up his "end," he picked it up in the middle.

All the fretting and sweating over being able to carry that load wasn't necessary. Grandpa knew my strength and the weight of that post all along. What I didn't know was grandpa's willingness and ability to carry most of my load.

Most of life's burdens with which one is faced are very much like that. We concentrate on our humanistic ability and burdens confronting us while forgetting the resources and reliability of our heavenly Father. If one is willing to pick up his own end of the burden, a close check will show God has already picked up his end—in the middle.

In the Bible our heavenly Father has made over seven thousand promises to his children. That many times he has said, in effect, pick up your share of life's burden and I'll pick up mine in the middle.

The anxiety and apprehension associated with most unknown and unexperienced burdens prompts many people to want to run from them. The shadowy image of individual inadequacy or inexperience is too often clearly in focus, while God's inventive ingenuity is ignored.

These shadows are often in the mind. That is where some of life's major battles are fought.

Dr. Nathan Kline, director of the Rockland State Hospital, remarked, "More human suffering has resulted from depression than any other single disease."

Dr. Smiley Blanton declared, "anxiety is the greatest modern plague. Thousands upon thousands of people either destroy their lives or frustrate them because of their preoccupation with anxiety, worry, and fear."

"Fear," said a distinguished psychologist, "is the most disintegrating factor in human personality."

Dr. Paul Tournier, a celebrated Swiss physician and psychiatrist, noted, "Most illnesses do not, as is generally thought, come like a bolt out of the blue. The ground is prepared for years, through faulty diet, intemperance, overwork, and moral conflicts, slowly eroding the subject's vitality. Man does not die, he kills himself. . . . Every act of physical, psychological, and moral disobedience of God's purpose is an act of wrong living and has its inevitable consequences."

An antidote for fear is proposed. In the house in Washington, D. C., across the street from Ford's Theater to which Abraham Lincoln was carried after an assassin shot him and where he died, is an old Bible reputed to be the one used by the President in the White House during the critical days of the (un) Civil War. A soiled indention, as though made by repeated application of the finger, is along the edge of the page on which is printed Psalm 34:4. The text states: "I sought the Lord, and he heard me, and delivered me from my fears." God is the source of complete freedom from fears.

Shakespeare's Henry VI observed, "True nobility is exempted from fear." The king of Kings affords his royal subjects a nobility of mind and heart which actually can exempt them from fear.

The Bible says love casts out fear. That's the key. Love gives confidence and motivation. If I had known then as I know now how very much Grandpa loved me, I would have had no fear of setting that post.

15 LOVE IT UP

The Shadow of Sex

> People who try to use eggs for baseball play short games. The same is true of people who try to use sex for what it cannot do.—Dr. Paul Barkman

> Love does not grow out of sex; love must grow into sex.—Walter Trobisch

> You cannot say that our physical body was made for sexual promiscuity; it was made for God, and God is the answer to our deepest longings.—1 Corinthians 6:13, Phillips

"We live in a Babylonian society perhaps more Babylonian than Babylon itself," says noted columnist Max Lerner.

"SEX" was the bold caption on a poster in a high school corridor. Some enterprising young candidate for student council office had posted it. The message was: "Now that I have your attention, please vote for. . . ." He knew how to attract interest.

In a more subtle, though often direct way, advertisers have capitalized on the topic. I saw a bold billboard which stated: "Saucey, Sassy, and Sexy." It was advertising shrimp. Sexy?

Buttons boast: "Revive fertility rights."

Bumper stickers state: "Love it up."

Magazines print: "Chaste makes waste."

Persons parrot: "Love thy neighbor, but don't get caught."

Psychologists such as Dr. Albert Ellis of New York brag: "We'll soon get virginity before marriage to the vanishing point, where it should be." Overt and covert efforts are being made to accomplish this objective.

Whereas the Puritans tended to deny sex, the present age pretends to defy it. We have shifted from acting as though sex did not exist to being obsessed with it. The Victorian personality sought to have love without falling into sex; the modern person seems to seek to have sex without falling into love. The sex goddess Diana is reincarnate. The moral guidelines that have steadied our society for centuries are eroded. God intended us to love people and use things. Now we love things and want to use people.

Western tradition has four types of love. One is sex, or what is called lust or libido. The second is eros, the drive of love to procreate or create. A third is philia, or friendship, brotherly love. The fourth is agape, the love that is devoted to others, the prototype of which is God's love for man. A radical shift in ideals has resulted in an overemphasis on the first type. There has been a virtual abandonment of the other three forms. Consequently, therapists rarely see patients who exhibit repression of sex. Because radical sexual freedom falls short of being fully human, therapists are seeing more persons with internal anxiety and guilt.

One caustic factor is the press. Russell J. Fornwalt observed, "It is said that more than fifteen million copies of 'girlie' magazines are bought every month in the United States. In a year's time, three billion copies of all kinds of pornographic publications—enough to fill to overflowing five Empire State Buildings—are purchased by adults and teenagers."

It is also reported that the sale of salacious magazines is twenty times that of all religious publications—Protestant, Catholic, and Jewish combined. And the National Citizens for Decent Literature says that 75 to 90 percent of all pornographic literature ends up in the hands of and, therefore, in the minds of, children.

The evidence justifying an indictment of our sex attitudes is mounting. Yale's Child Study Center reports that there are over three hundred thousand children born out of wedlock each year. Divorces resulting from extra-marital affairs are approaching one in four. "Birthright" estimates over four thousand abortions a week are performed in America.

Dr. Francis J. Braceland, former president of the American Psychiatric Association, says, "Pre-marital sex relations resulting from the so-called new morality have greatly increased the number of young people in mental hospitals."

Dr. Eric Fromm, the internationally noted psychoanalyst, said the current sexual freedoms in no way contribute to a true sense of aliveness or richness of experience. There is a frustrating emptiness which follows.

When sex is stripped of love and drained of its intended meaning, it turns to exert explosive stress on the personality. I have observed a set pattern of promiscuity. First there is great excitement and pleasure in it. Then one partner begins feeling guilty. Next, embarrassment, shame, and hate develop. Finally, they break up and become enemies.

Often this is as varied as one partner merely deserting the other. In instances where more sexual licenses are allowed, the idea of marriage emerges. Sexual freedom normally prompts the girl to think more and more about marriage, and the boy to think less and less about it. The male has a tendency to lose interest in long-range goals as a result of pre-marital sexual attainment. The female response is one of endearment.

Franz Winkler, German-born, New York psychiatrist, related that his case studies belie the statement that pre-marital sex is advisable preparation for marriage. His conclusion was that the more satisfactory the pre-marital sex relation the more unsatisfactory the marital sex relation. He stated psychological mental blocks growing out of guilt and suspicion as the cause.

Dr. Mervyn Sanders concurs with these conclusions in his book, "Medical Aspects of Human Sexuality." He observed, "If individuals proceed to prove mechanical compatibility which is body to body, which is less than 1% of the problem, they endanger psychological compatibility, which is more than 99% in the process." Sex, particularly to the female, is more than physical. It is intended to be the zenith expression of genuine love. It was never intended to be an end in itself, but a means to an end. There are two primary intended reasons for sex. One is for propagation and the other is loving commitment through intimate involvement.

One's experiences in marriage are interpreted by the occurrences in courtship. Promiscuity before marriage causes mistrust in marriage. Sexual license before marriage results in suspicion in marriage. Conversely, virtue, patience, and protectiveness before marriage consequent in confidence, love, and assurance in marriage.

Will James, psychologist and philosopher, reminds us the past is ever present with us. "Nothing we ever do is in the strict scientific literalness wiped out. Down among your nerve cells and fibers, the molecules are counting it, registering and scoring it up to be used against you when the next temptation comes. Could the young but realize how soon they will become walking bundles of habits! We are spinning our own fates, good or evil. We are imitators and copiers of our past selves."

Dr. Smiley Blanton, a well-known psychiatrist, stressed the importance of winning over temptation. "Every day of your life, no matter how sheltered you are, you face some choice in which the wrong action is so seductive, so plausible, so pleasurable that it takes a conscious act of the will to reject it. Temptation is universal, as old as the Garden of Eden. Much of your happiness or unhappiness depends on your ability to handle it—instead of letting it handle you." Note he says it takes "a conscious act of the will" to overcome temptation. That is, there must be a decision before deception in order that there might be discretion.

The best time to make a decision is before you have to make it. Reaching a conclusion is more effective and accurate when there is no pressure that causes emotions to override objectivity. That is exactly when most decisions are made. The implementation follows.

A lovely, pregnant, unwed mother sat in my office repeating, "I don't know why I did it." She responded indignantly when I said, "You did it because you decided in

advance you would." I explained that by the music to which
she listened, books and magazines she read, movies she
viewed, and by her own thoughts, she decided in advance.
Reluctantly, but willfully, she acknowledged that to be
correct. In simple summary, if you don't intend to go in
the house, stay off the front porch.

There are inevitable consequences of sexual promiscuity
that cannot be prevented by penicillin or abortion.
Clarence McCartney's statement attests to this truth: "The
laws of God are given for man's good and perfection, and
wherever violated they bring suffering. Prophylactics may
save from physical disease; and contraceptives from children; but there is no prophylactic which can save the mind
from contamination or the soul from tarnish, and there
is no contraceptive which will prevent the conception of
children of regret, self-despising, and self-degradation."

In addition to these individual personal warnings against
promiscuity, there are collective public alerts. Two noted
historians have spoken regarding national moral decay and
the inevitable consequence.

Arnold Toynbee based his observations on the study
analysis of nineteen formerly great civilizations. He noted,
"No nation has ever survived that failed to discipline itself
sexually."

Edith Hamilton, specialist in Greek history, made a
summary comment regarding the land that gave birth to
Hedonism. (The New Morality is a synonym for Hedonism.) "When the freedom they wished for most was the
freedom from responsibility, then Athens ceased to be free,
and was never free again."

Personal and collective steps need to be taken at once

in order to safeguard our future. Certain advantageous moves are advisable.

A young man went out of church quoting the minister's statement on sex: "Remember, sex was God's idea, not mine." The youth failed to complete the thought which continued: "Likewise, don't forget he also has an ideal for sex." The ideal is that it is proper. The persons and conditions are the key. The ideal is for it to be an expression of love between a husband and wife with lasting consequence. Anything, ANYTHING, other than that is less than that.

"It is time to wake up to reality. . . . Let us therefore fling away the things that men do in the dark; let us arm ourselves for the fight of the day! Let us live cleanly, as in the daylight, not in the 'delights' of getting drunk or playing with sex. Let us be Christ's men from head to foot, and give no chance to the flesh to have its fling" (Rom. 13:11-14, Phillips)

The following attitudes lead one to the fulfillment of God's ideal for sex:

1. Abdication of sex from the throne of your life is a starting point. It is a fulfilling servant in marriage, but a demanding master out of marriage.

2. Accept persons as complete beings. Never think of anyone as merely a body.

3. Acknowledge that every close friendship between persons of opposite sex does not have to end in sex relations.

4. Avoid temptation. Flee youthful lust. Be mindful that "youthful lust" lingers even when the body has grown older. Expect temptation.

5. Account for the consequences. Remember that to sow to the wind is to reap the consequences.

6. Avow never to use or flaunt yourself in the game of lust. Don't play with volatile explosives.

7. Advance commitment is essential. Pledge to be in thought what you want to be in act.

8. Allow God's word to be your guide.

"God's plan is to make you holy, and that entails first of all a clean cut with sexual immorality. Every one of you should learn to control his body, keeping it pure and treating it with respect, and never regarding it as an instrument for self-gratification, as do pagans with no knowledge of God. You cannot break this rule without in some way cheating your fellow men. It is not for nothing that the Spirit God gives us is called the Holy Spirit. Avoid sexual looseness like the plague! Every other sin that a man commits is done outside his own body. Have you forgotten that your body is the temple of the Holy Spirit, Who lives in you and is God's gift to you, and that you are not the owner of your own body? You have been bought, and at what a price! Therefore, bring glory to God in your body" (1 Thess. 4:3-6; 1 Cor. 6:18-20, Phillips).

16 IT CAME TO PASS

The Shadow of Time

> Dost thou love life? Then do not squander time, for that is the stuff life is made of.—Benjamin Franklin

> Blessed are the methodical for they do not waste time, and time is the stuff life is made of.—*Arkansas Methodist*

> Redeeming the time, because the days are evil.—Ephesians 5:16

"Time marches on!" That by-line for the news of the world intrigues me. Before a lot of people realize that time is marching toward them, most of it has passed. The relativity of time was called to my attention by an inscription I saw on a large clock in Switzerland.

> When as a child I laughed and wept,
>   Time crept.
> When as a youth, I dreamed and talked,
>   Time walked.
> When I became a full grown man,
>   Time ran.
> When older still I grew,
>   Time flew.
> Soon I shall find in traveling on,
>   Time gone.

The author of that verse is unknown, but the truth it represents is not. Each person is in one of those groups described.

99

We do well to write on our heart that today will be the best day of our life. Don't rush by today to get to tomorrow. Do not anticipate some future event so much that you waste today. Likewise, don't be like a peacock whose glory is behind. To live a past tense life is never to move into today's world.

The story is told of an early Southerner who misinterpreted a passage of Scripture and still got value from it. When asked his favorite verse he replied:

"My favorite verse in da Bible is da one what say, 'It come to pass.' Ever time something bad come along I don't worry none cause I know it done come to pass. Ever time something good come along I enjoy it all I can cause I know it too done come to pass."

Nearly five thousand years ago man noted in Sanskrit the value of time. "Look well to this one day, for it and it alone is life. In the brief course of this one day lie all the verities and realities of your existence; the pride of growth, the glory of action, the splendor of beauty. Yesterday is only a dream and tomorrow is but a vision. Yet, each day, well lived, makes every yesterday a dream of happiness and each tomorrow a vision of hope. Look well, therefore, to this one day, for it and it alone is life."

Mankind has long known those facts. Unfortunately few have ever learned the lessons. Those who have are the producers. Gladstone, a former prime minister of Britain, acknowledged it by saying: "Believe me when I tell you that thrift of time will repay you with a profit beyond your most sans gene dreams; and that waste of it will make you dwindle alike in intellectual and moral stature, beyond your darkest reckoning."

"Never put off until tomorrow what you can do today." That old bromide was spoon fed to most of us in youth. Its origin is known by few. Philip Dormer Stanhope, the Earl of Chesterfield, originally stated: "Know the true value of time. Snatch it, seize it, enjoy every second of it. No laziness, no idleness, no procrastination; never put off until tomorrow what you can do today."

I have never met a person, who was successful, who did not know the value of time. Such a one is punctual, productive, and an anti-procrastinator. He has the capacity to capture the charm of each day.

Sand can't flow upward in an hourglass. Once set, the sun cannot rise in the West. Therefore, trade every minute for something significant. There are no reruns or instant replays. Ring every drop of duty from each deed and every ounce of energy out of every day. Destroy laziness with action. Dispel doubt with faith. Displace hate with love. Dismember fear with confidence.

On a sixth-grade bulletin board I saw the following: "Today is God's gift to you. What you do with it is your gift to him." His gifts are good. Let's be sure ours are good for something. To misuse a day is to reject a gift. To waste a day may be to mar the last day of your life. Schedule your time wisely—discipline your use of it.

Each year places at our disposal 8,756 hours. Of these 2,920 hours will be spent in sleep. That leaves 5,836 hours on which to build your dreams. Those hours provide:

> Time to work—
> it is the price of success.
> Time to reason—
> it is the source of power.

Time to play—
it is the perpetuator of youth.
Time to read—
it is the touchstone of wisdom.
Time to worship—
it is the soul's refreshment.
Time to be friendly—
it is the way to happiness.
Time to dream—
it is setting one's sights on a star.
Time to love in Christ's name—
it is the way to gratification.

The opening verses of John's Gospel inform us that time was part of creation. When creation is considered, most often physical objects come to mind. The sun, moon, stars, and planets flash into mind. A literal translation of John's opening communique is: "Before time began to begin." Thus, the picture is of time as not being in a period past. Time itself was created at a particular point.

The writer of the Revelation informs his readers that there will be a day when "time shall be no more." The Bible pictures time as both beginning and ending. Mankind is in a parentheses between eternity past and eternity future.

Eternity? Yes, eternity! Einstein pointed us toward a better theory of eternity than most theologians. His formula $E = mc_2$ opened a new concept of time. An imaginary trip can illustrate the variableness of time. An ultra-high-speed rocket voyage, at about the speed of light (186,000 miles per second) to Sirius, nine light years away, reveals some startling facts. At this speed one's watch, heart, respiration, and digestion would slow down by a factor of

70,000. Consequently, the eighteen-year roundtrip would require little food.

Twelve hours would elapse by your watch. However, upon returning, your friends here on earth would be eighteen years older. If acceleration equaled the speed of light, time would stand still. The heart would stop beating, but you would not die. You would be capsuled in "now."

Recently I looked back in history over one million years. I looked at the Andromeda Galaxy through a telescope at Fernbank Science Center. It is about a million-and-a-half light years away. That means that the light I saw from Andromeda left there over a million years ago. Looking with the naked eye at the nearest star, Alpha Centauri, one sees into the past by over five hundred years.

Reverse the vantage points. Suppose one were on the star Sirius looking back at planet earth with a telescope. What would be seen would be what happened nine years ago. In a scientific sense, from the perspective of Sirius, you are now doing what you did nine years ago.

Therefore, from some celestial vantage point everything is in the eternal now. Heaven is the place where this eternal stage exists.

When the bright and shining angel will announce time shall be no more is not known. The fact that he will do it is known. Peter described the event. "It remains true that the day of the Lord will come as suddenly and unexpectedly as a thief. In that day the heavens will disappear in a terrific blast; the very elements will disintegrate in the heat and the earth and all that is in it will be burned up to nothing . . . our hopes are set not on these, but on the new heavens, and the new earth which he has

promised us, and in which nothing but good shall live"
(2 Pet. 3:10-12, Phillips).

Thomas E. Murray, while a member of the Atomic
Energy Commission, commented: "It may be the inscruta-
ble will of God to make the twentieth century closing time
for the human race."

For the person, who by faith in Christ is ready for time
to run out, that's the end—the front end of an eternal life.

As a former Boy Scout, I commend the spiritual value
of their motto: Be Prepared.

17 THE QUALITY GENERATION

The Shadow of Youth

> Truthfulness is a cornerstone in character, and if it be not firmly laid in youth there will ever after be a weak spot in the foundation.—Jefferson Davis

> Always, when given the necessary guidance and opportunity, youth has shown that it can produce the requisite know-how. Age, on the other hand, is often over tenacious and temperamentally unwilling to cede the power it has acquired.—Felix Morley, *Nation's Business*

> Rejoice, O young man, in thy youth; and let thy heart cheer thee in the days of thy youth, and walk in the ways of thine heart, and in the sight of thine eyes.—Ecclesiastes 11:9

"I'd rather try to cool off a volcano than to heat up an iceberg," said the executive head of a large firm.

Today's volcano seems to be youth. It is one thing no one need run from. Rapidly it runs away from us. This frightens some persons into overindulgence in use of synthetics to try to maintain a youthful look. Youth is the hottest commodity on the modern market.

Conversely, many adults serve as judge and jury ready to indict youth for the "crime" of being young.

One reason Granny puts young people down for the way they dress is that old pictures, of her dressed very much like them during the Coolidge administration, keep popping up.

Grandpa, having forgotten Buffalo Bill and his peers wore their hair long as a gesture of defiance of the Indians, often makes getting a haircut a test of fellowship.

Unisex was big on campus in the twenties. It surely

wasn't called that. He's and she's wore yellow slickers, coonskin coats, and four-buckle galoshers.

External fads change and are yet always alike. Isn't this descriptive: "They reversed the traditional order of things even in trivial matters of external appearance, the males allowed their hair to grow long and the females adopted cutting it short, and adding sometimes the additional blue badge of blue spectacles." That was a description given of youth by a writer in 1880.

Atlantic Monthly reported:

Antagonism between generations seems to be inevitable and may as well be recognized and dealt with, not denied and smoothed over, just because we wish that it did not exist. The old and the young are as far apart in point of view, code and standard, as if they belonged to different races. A different language is spoken in both cases; the morality is different; the temperaments are divided by a channel as wide as the Straits of Dover; the ideals are not the same; the sense of humor, the sense of taste, and the scale of values are totally dissimilar. . . . Let us frankly, if regretfully, accept as a premise that the two generations are natural enemies, suspicious of each other, critical, distrustful, unsympathetic, and hostile.

That by-line was dated 1922.

Philosopher George Santayana was aghast that same year because of students who "all proclaim their disgust with the present state of things in America; they denounce the Constitution of the United States, the churches, the colleges, the press . . . they are against everything—but what are they for? I have not been able to discover."

The following is a clipping from the *New York Times.*

For the past ten years I have been a close observer of what has passed among the rising generation in this great metropolis

(New York City), and I cannot suppress the humiliating conviction that even pagan Rome never witnessed more rapid and frightful declension in morals, nor witnessed among certain classes of young a more utter disregard for honor, truth, piety, and even the commonest decencies of life.

The date on that by-line was January 1865.

The year half the senior class at Harvard was expelled as were half the student body at Princeton the press reported: "Nassau Hall resounded to the reports of pistols and the crash of bricks against doors, walls, and windows."

The students at Yale and Virginia were not to be outdone. They violently protested "stupid courses," examinations, politics, bad food, religion, and morals.

Those events are not remembered because they happened shortly after 1806.

The following sounds much more current.

"Our earth is degenerate; bribery and corruption are common; children no longer obey their parents; every man wants to write his memoirs."

Those words were impressed on an Assyrian clay tablet dated around 2800 B.C.

These quotes are not recited as an endorsement of such conduct nor to encourage it. They are merely evidences that no generation of young people has ever been satisfied with the world as they found it. They want to change it.

Many of them have a word other than change. The president of a senior class for which I was delivering the commencement address said, "We do not merely want to change the world. That might imply destructiveness. We want to improve the world." This constructive, creative desire is the desire of many. With all their brass and brashness, they are to be preferred any day to spiritless adults with little sense of mission in life. This "Earthrise Generation" is different from others only in that they are better educated, more energetic, and better fed. They have had the opportunity of being born at a wonderful period of history. I speak now of that segment of the youth culture that deserves to be referred to as "The Quality Generation."

Many youth have resolved that this is no time to recline. They are not willing to become a mutation of their more meaningful self. They know they were born an original and they have no desire to die a blurred, cheap, carbon copy of someone else. They do not want to consent to commonplaceness by reclining to the lowest common denominator. May their number multiply.

Many youth have decided that this is no time to whine. These are not the complainers, who demand permanent residence in "fat city" in order to keep their cool. They accept the demanding challenge of life uncomplainingly. They still get a lift from scintillating meaningful morality, stimulating spirituality, and super-scholarship. They are willing to do the job at hand without complaint.

Many of these same youth have decided that this is a time to incline. By the thousands they are inclining their lives toward Christ. Never has there been such a large percentage of the youthful population so dedicated and informed of Bible truths. The evidences of their commitment consists of more than an upraised index finger. It is evidenced by an uplifted and uplifting life.

One of the nation's most sought after young athletes and I talked together in the basement of my residence until 1:00 A.M. We concluded with prayer by his request and my desire. As he left he said, "Pastor, let's the two of us keep on praying about this and the three of us will settle it." Such was the personal nature of Christ to this young man that he knew of his presence. To such young people Christ is more than a nostalgic memory, an abstract theory, a bloodless philosophy, or a historical character. He is a living present friend who makes a difference.

Adolph Hitler said, "The Hitler youth will be our salvation."

Karl Marx said, "For ultimate victory win the young mind."

Dr. Pusey, President of Harvard University, said, "The young people of today are looking for a creed to believe, a song to sing, and a flag to follow."

J. Edgar Hoover said, "If America is to remain a Christian nation, then more adults must assume the responsibility of preparing young Americans for virile, dynamic, Christian living."

The best lessons of life are caught not taught. Practice and precept are both tutors. Adults have a distinct opportunity to help develop youth. The day of deception is over. They want performance as well as profession. Look out! Someone is looking in.

Centuries ago a teenager named Daniel reached a decision in Babylon. He was away from home. There were no friends to report on him. The pressure was forceful to violate his convictions. Of him it is written, "Daniel purposed in his heart not to defile himself." Note the emphasis on self-will. That single youthful decision changed the course of two civilizations.

Many today have dropped out of the "Playboy" bunny race, quit the Hefner pleasure chase, and avoided society's money haste to follow Christ.

The following are a few who have resolved to "Let no man despise thy youth, but be thou an example of believers, in word, in conversation, in charity, in spirit, in faith, in purity" (1 Tim. 4:12).

Pete Pifer, Oregon State, All-American: "I have found that the excitement of following Christ is without comparison."

Tim Carter, UCLA varsity baseball: "It's so satisfying to see Christ work out his plan in my life."

Jan Elliot, Pi Beta Phi, University of Oklahoma: "God loves me and has changed my life. My total happiness is in him."

John Klein, Minnesota's wrestling co-captain: "Christ did not make me the best wrestler in the nation, but one of the happiest."

Larry Gonzales, student body president, Florida State University: "I've learned that the Christian life is an exciting and challenging one."

These young people use a delightful array of synonyms for kicks—exciting, challenging, happiness, and satisfying.

As I look over my shoulder and see the volcano of the youth erupting, I have no desire to try to cool them off. They excite my imagination. They just might warm up the iceberg that is representative of many adults.

18 A WRINKLED SKIN WITHOUT A SHRIVELED SOUL

The Shadow of Age

> As I approve of a youth that has something of the old man in him, so I am no less pleased with an old man that has something of the youth. He that follows this rule may be old in body, but can never be so in mind.—Cicero

> One thing is a comfort to my old age—that none of my works . . . contain a line I would wish to blot out, because of pandering to the baser passions of nature. This is a comfort to me; I can do no mischief by my works when I am gone.—William Wordsworth

> So we do not lose heart. Though our outer nature is wasting away, our inner nature is being renewed every day.—2 Corinthians 4:16

Father Time outruns the swiftest young sprinter. He even caught Ponce de Leon before he found the much sought after Fountain of Youth. The most avid eater of Vitamin E cannot elude him. Exercise buffs have no success in stopping his methodical march.

Solomon once gave a graphic description of the aging process.

"the keepers of the house shall tremble." (Hands shake.)

"the strong men shall bow themselves down." (Legs grow weak.)

"the grinders cease because they are few." (Teeth decay.)

"those that look out the windows be darkened." (Vision fails.)

"the sound of the grinding is low." (Digestion is poor.)

"he shall rise up at the voice of a bird." (Insomnia.)

"the daughters of music shall be brought low." (Hearing impaired.)

"fears shall be in the way." (Phobias develop.)

"the almond tree shall flourish." (Hair turns grey.)

"desire shall fail." (Sexual impotence.)

"the golden bowl be broken." (Cerebral difficulty.)

"the pitcher be broken at the fountain." (Heart trouble.)

"the wheel broken at the cistern." (Blood pressure problems.)

"Then shall the dust return to the earth as it was: and the spirit shall return unto the God who gave it" (Eccl. 12:3-7).

If that seems like an unpleasant prospect, consider the alternative—dying young. The subtle pastels of Solomon's painting are more beautiful in that light.

The possibility of eluding age permanently is nil. Nevertheless, the prospect of delaying it is fun. Some aids to evasiveness are: proper lifelong diet, avoidance of harmful rays of the sun (i.e., gamma and X-rays) which cause aging, consistent exercise, and good hygiene.

The Veterans Administration recently reported that in twenty-five years the average life expectancy likely will be 120. An essential is the raising of the age of retirement to 100. Their conclusion is, people live only as long as they are needed. A sense of dignity resulting from a feeling of productivity is essential.

An orchid found in a trash can is still an orchid. Therefore, the wisdom of Nietzsche is worth observing: "Whoever has a reason for living endures almost any mode of life." Establish your reason. Make it demanding. The result will be fulfilling. Purpose is important.

In order to increase and maintain such a purpose in life, certain things are needful. It helps to keep a number of creative short term projects going. These projects should require time and energy. Hobbies are good. Learn new ones.

No one grows old by simply living a certain number

of years. People grow old when they desert their ideals. Gaining age may wrinkle the skin, but the loss of interest shrivels the soul. In the control center of every life there is a computer; so long as it receives messages of hope, love, joy, faith, and courage, the person is young. When the snow of pessimism and the frost of negativism down the wires, then one grows old.

Spending time with one's peers is wise. This should not be done exclusively, but discretely. Remember, to stay young, stay with young people. To die young, try to keep up with them.

An awareness of the asset of accumulated wisdom gives a sense of worth. Do not speak to every subject. Let it be known, however, that many truths are spoken through false teeth.

The fifth of the Ten Commandments states an often overlooked factor. It is the basic principle that honoring of one's parents is rewarded by longevity. This is the first Command with promise. Numerous, personally observed cases confirm this concept. There evidently is something much more therapeutic about it than is known. Respect of parents is so highly thought of by God that he offers a blessing for it.

Abraham Lincoln advised: "You are as old as your fears and as young as your hopes." Keep hope alive. Hope is a word that carries a double punch. Originally it meant desire plus expectation. A driving desire to achieve a certain goal is catalyzing. When this is coupled with an expectancy there is an air of excitement. Desire plus expectation perpetuates youthfulness.

Henry David Thoreau commented: "None are so old

as those who have outlived enthusiasm." Persons should not wait until age is upon them to develop this capacity. It is more easily developed in youth. It becomes a carrying characteristic in age. Don't ever let the child-like vivaciousness within your nature die. Give vent to excitement over successes. Show elation over accomplishments. Evidence a zeal for life. Demonstrate a determination to achieve. Never give up.

Many persons have done their most productive work when they have passed the normal retirement age.

Pablo Picasso, past seventy-five, dominated the art world.

Socrates learned to play a musical instrument after his hair whitened with the snow of age.

Grandma Moses began her art career at seventy-nine.

Chaucer's "Canterbury Tales" were written during his latter years.

Goethe wrote "Faust" when past eighty.

Cato began his study of Greek and Plutarch his study of Latin when they were eighty.

George Bernard Shaw was still writing plays at ninety.

Theophrastus began "The Character of Man," his greatest work, on his ninetieth birthday.

Frank Lloyd Wright at ninety was still considered the most creative architect of his time.

Arnauld translated the historical works of Josephus when he was eighty.

Michaelangelo did some of his best painting after the age of eighty.

Titian was still painting masterpieces when he was ninety-eight.

Chevreul, the French scientist, was keen and energetic at the age of 103.

Oliver Wendell Holmes at ninety resigned from the United States Supreme Court. Upon visiting the retired Justice, President Franklin Roosevelt found him reading Plato. The President inquired, "Why Plato?" Holmes replied, "To improve my mind, Mr. President."

These persons verify Emerson's observation: "We need not count a man's years until he has nothing else to count."

Growing old gracefully is an often used adage. It is an admirable goal. There are few persons as pleasant to be around as a well disciplined child and a graceful older person. Charm is not a coat to be adorned suddenly. It is developed. The following are ten steps to aging admirably.

1. Learn to smile and shrug. Demonstrate that you don't take yourself too seriously. Most awkward incidents are not as important as they might seem at first. A smile brightens the road for others. A shrug lightens the load for yourself.

2. Control your voice. Volume as well as inflection are important. The way one says something often communicates more than the words used. Resolve to use pleasant and kind remarks.

3. Keep your mind open. Be receptive to new thoughts, programs, and insights. Please learn that you are never too old to learn. Be a good listener. This will cause most people to think you are a good conversationalist.

4. Avoid being critical as though it is a plague. "Walk A Mile in My Shoes" is not only good music, but good medicine. Always anticipate the best. Compliment that

which is worthy.

5. Bury all grudges before they bury you. Don't treat a grudge like it is your most treasured possession. Bitterness hurts only the one who is bitter. It evidences that someone else controls your temperament. Assert your independent temperament by not dwelling on a grudge.

6. Never insist on being authoritative about everything. Don't demand to have the last word. Apologies are never necessary for improper words unspoken.

7. Resolve to make the best of your plight. Self-pity is a corroding acid. It eats up energy and initiative. Count your many blessings. Don't dwell on your liabilities. Accept the fact that you, like everybody else, have them.

8. Evidence courage and confidence in today. Avoid fear of the future because of its blinding effect. Never take council of your fears. Displace fear with cheer. Have confidence in your assets.

9. Keep your eyes on the future. Never exaggerate on how good things used to be. Be a citizen of the current culture. Apply life's lessons to today's world.

10. Put your faith in Jesus Christ. Bet your life for time and eternity on him. Practice the joy of his presence. Loneliness is avoided by realizing he is with you. Don't act like he is with you—act because he is with you.

One's mind-set is important in athletics and the academic. It is more important in aging. Many older persons suffer from "give-up-itis." Years before, they decided they would give up on life at a certain age. They preset the time to give up their will to live. As a self-fulfillment, that age brings death or inactivity. That standard can be revised. A sense of need, hope, and enthusiasm are paddles to get us up that stream.

Resolve with Henry Van Dyke:

> "I shall grow old, but
> Never lose life's zest,
> Because the road's last turn,
> Will be the best."

19 POOR OLE SAM PASSED ON

The Shadow of Death

> When I go down to the grave I can say, like so many others, I have finished my work; but I cannot say I have finished my life. My day's work will begin the next morning. My tomb is not a blind alley. It is a thoroughfare. It closes in the twilight to open in the dawn.—Victor Hugo

> To the Christian, death has redemptive significance. It is the portal through which we enter the presence of our Lord.—Hilys Jasper

> O death, where is thy sting? O grave, where is thy victory?—1 Corinthians 15:55

I was scared to death of death. Then I realized that death died the day Jesus Christ arose from the grave. He turned a death dirge into a day of delight, and transformed a funeral into a festival. That event dispels the old shadow cast by an ancient inquiry, "If a man die shall he live again?" As certainly as that "if" means "when," the "shall" means "he will."

Fear of death has been classified as one of the basic fears of life. Behind the fear of death is a lack of understanding of life. Tolstoy once said, "I hate life but I am afraid to die."

The seventeenth-century philosopher Blaise Pascal wrote, "Since men could not do away with death, they decided not to think about it." The fact is man has always thought about it but seldom had nerve enough to talk about it. The subtle old taboo against thinking and talking about death is vanishing with some good and some bad results.

118

A German churchman noted that pornography and voyeurism surfaced as the old time sex taboo was being overcome. There also are present dangers of a "pornography of death" and "voyeurism of violence." Modern movies and current comedy hint at this.

Death certificates were given out at the Indiana Catholic Conference and participants were urged to fill them out speculating about their own death. The aim was stated to be to "put people in touch with their own feelings about dying."

At the University of Cincinnati students were urged to visit funeral homes and cemeteries to get the "feel" of them. At the University of Minnesota students have tried out coffins and theoretically planned their own funerals. One teacher said the students found that death "is not morbid, but exciting, dynamic."

One hippie, observing a wealthy man being buried in a Cadillac limousine, was overheard to say, "What a way to go!"

All of these approaches are attempts to do to death what has basically been done to life—make it humanistic. The physical aspect is emphasized in each instance—much thought for the body but none for the soul.

Elizabeth Kubler-Ross describes five basic stages through which one goes if he is confronted with advance knowledge of his death. These stages are: denial and isolation, anger, bargaining, depression, and acceptance. If persons could gain a wholesome acceptance of death's meaning and inevitability the other stages might be avoided.

The resurrection of Christ gives death its proper perspective for the Christian. Friends of a deceased Christian can stand by the casket and think not that he is there, but thank God he is there—heaven. They can rejoice not that he is gone, but that he has arrived in heaven.

The Scripture speaks of the Lord giving and the Lord taking away. The victory is in knowing that God has not ghoulishly taken away from us, but he has graciously "taken" unto himself. Biblically there seem to be only three reasons Christians die.

One is that the person has finished his earthly mission and God allows him to come on home and be rewarded. A full life cannot be determined by chronology, but by character.

A second reason is martyrdom that advances the cause of Christ. On each continent this has been dramatically noted in each generation.

The third reason is that the Christian has sinned the "sin unto death." This means his conduct has so impaired his witness that his death will bring more glory to God than his unrepentant life.

Death, like all events of life, is not a goal, but a gateway. It is a means to an end. To most normal people there is apprehension associated with the idea of dying. This is a wholesome preservative for life. Apparently, a part of God's grace is that when the moment of death comes for a Christian the fear is removed. The psalmist said, "Yea, though I walk through the valley of the shadow of death I will fear no evil." There is no fear because God is with "me."

When persons realize that God is present with them in life, they grow to accept the fact of his presence at the time of death. Thus, denial and isolation, anger, bargaining, and depression are aborted.

I wanted to turn and walk away from a hospital room door. A brokenhearted husband, for whom I was waiting, had just come from the room where the doctor had told his wife she had terminal cancer. I knew she would emerge any moment and I awkwardly did not know what to expect. Momentarily she came out. She was radiant. Fresh makeup almost concealed her dried tears. She spoke cheerfully and apologetically for disturbing our luncheon plans. Then she noted, "I've lived all of my life in preparation for this, therefore, I am ready to go home." She did go to her ultimate home within a few weeks, rejoicing.

The Bible speaks of the body as a "tabernacle." A tabernacle was the equivalent of a pup tent. Pup tents are not permanent dwellings. They provide temporary housing only. Jesus spoke of going to prepare a place for his followers in his Father's house of many mansions. When the Christian dies, he merely moves from temporary housing in a pup tent (body) into the mansion (heaven). That is a fantastic spiritual real estate transaction.

This is a swift move. The expression Paul used is, "To be absent from the body is to be present with the Lord." If a modern teenager were transliterating that it would mean, "The instant you die you are eyeball to eyeball with God."

That long shadow called death is removed by life—eternal life.

"Dust thou art and unto dust shalt thou return" was not spoken of the soul. That is a summary of death as a gateway to glory. Be sure you are ready.

The summary of life will someday be inscribed on your grave. May it embody the truth on the tomb of George Washington:

"A sincere Christian doing all things for the will of his Master and resting his hope of eternal happiness alone on the righteousness of Jesus Christ."

Life after death for Christians is the highest form conceivable. Somewhere I once heard it said that if all fetuses in all wombs of all women of all the world could communicate, at the birth of one of them named Sam, the others would be heard to say—"Poor ole Sam passed on."